A Journey on Borrowed Time

By
Robert Russell Allen

Strategic Book Group

Strategic Book Group
P.O. Box 333
Durham CT 06422
www.StrategicBookClub.com

ISBN: 978-1-60911-936-2

Design: Dedicated Business Solutions, Inc. (www.netdbs.com)

A Journey on
Borrowed Time

Introduction

This is a story that I would invite you to concentrate on the similarities you find rather than trying to identify with the specifics that may easily differ from your life experience. If you honestly try to identify with me, you are bound to embark on a life-changing journey. The specifics of my life are not as relevant as the generalities and the feelings associated with those events. If you remain open to hear what my story really tells, then you are ready to begin the journey that will prompt you to think you are reading a fantasy, when in fact it is a true story. I would also ask you not to consider the term *alcoholism* as you begin, because that word and concept were unknown to me as I began my life experience. It did not play into my thinking, nor did it affect my actions in any way for decades to follow. Perhaps you, or someone close and important to you, will benefit from my experience and come away with some insights not easily learned along normal life pathways. This is a true story of endurance, survival, and success with the help of Alcoholics Anonymous. A journey that begins in innocence, staggers forward through six decades, and ends up teetering on the brink of death not once, but many times. Let me take you back in time, starting in my early teen years when we did not know what is common knowledge to our teens today. For me this was the mid-1950s, and I was being raised by my parents, who were a loving and stable couple, and a sister who was two years older than me. It was an age of innocence—an era in which most family matters were considered personal and confidential.

There was no crime in my small community. The politics were of a nation united by patriotism and harmony among most Americans. Matters of sexuality and close personal relations were not discussed because of the embarrassment it caused among gentle people. I had learned a few things about sexuality from my friends in the neighborhood and at school, but I didn't really know what to believe. Since I often rode my bike, played with my dog, or adventured into the nearby woods to act like a cowboy or pretend I was hunting, I had little reason to ask the questions that would have taught me more about life. I was more comfortable alone than being with any number of people. The young girls were okay, just a bit of a mystery to me, and I had no idea what to think about my feelings. At this point in my life, I was much the same as my peers blindly putting one foot in front of the other, simply wondering what might be ahead. It wasn't long before I began to recognize the turning points in my life that usually came with some pain. My parents didn't mention that life was not going to go smoothly because life is life, something we all learn as time goes by.

Table of Contents

CHAPTER 1

My Biggest Turning Point

"Autoclave Twelve, Autoclave Twelve! This is Dust Off Five, Dust Off Five, over!"

The static and the voice of the medical evacuation helicopter pilot were of equal volume on the radio, but there was no mistaking the tension in the pilot's voice.

"Autoclave Twelve, do you copy?"

The medical technicians of the 12th Evacuation Hospital in Cu Chi, Vietnam, rushed to the radio to reassure the pilot they were ready to hear him. "Dust Off Five, Dust Off Five! This is Autoclave Twelve. Go!"

"Autoclave, I'm about three miles out and closing fast on your location! Over!"

"Dust Off Five, what have you got? Over."

"Autoclave, I've got a VSI (very seriously injured) on board that needs you bad!" The pilot's voice never hesitated. The sound of the static from the radio and the helicopter blades cutting through the humid air could not disguise the urgency of his call. "I'm going to need some extra help when I land!"

"Dust Off Five, I'm sending some extra men and a doc for you to our pad. The landing zone is clear for your VSI! Over."

"Autoclave, my guys are having trouble holding this one down on the litter because of his pain. His legs are bad! Over."

"Dust Off Five, we'll be there for you buddy; just put her down on our pad! Over."

"Autoclave, I'm less than two minutes out!"

1

This was the third of February, 1967, and would prove to be a day remembered by many whose lives came crashing together at this emergency clinic during the Vietnam War. Some of their family members would not learn about this event for several days; some would not learn for many years. One man died, one man withdrew into his own mind, and one man's post-traumatic stress from this event would fuel his alcoholism for decades to come. I was the last and the lesser injured of those three. Others would carry their memories all the remaining days of their lives. No one escaped that day without scares! No one.

"Autoclave Twelve, this is Dust Off Five. He's all yours, pal, good luck!"

Nothing in my basic training had prepared me to suddenly jump into the mix of combat casualties and pretend not to see the horror all around. I believe my mind paused and held some of the information from entering. Overload. Disbelief. Fear.

Everything kept moving even though I had mentally stopped. The pictures kept changing, and the noises continued to batter me. I had to keep moving, keep helping where I could.

**

In elementary school, I had written notes and talked to the young ladies in my classes and considered several of them friends. I remember liking them better than the boys because they were more predictable, and I was rarely comfortable with the usual roughhousing that occurred while playing with the boys. I was slender and had not toughened up in my early years. I enjoyed few sports. When junior high school rolled around, I started to play football and finally began to grow as a young man. During this time, my interest in having a girlfriend was also blossoming, but my shyness held me back from actively trying to advance a friendship. Because I was fifteen years old, my interest was growing, but I didn't have the courage to press forward. Confidence eluded me; I was still the kid from the hilltop cottage who kept to himself.

During the ninth grade, I needed a minor medical procedure on my foot, and while in the hospital, my room was visited by student nurses giggling and trying to get my attention, making me blush. In the end it was all talk. Nothing happened except that I buried my feelings and moved backward on the social ladder. When I was sixteen and in my first year at the high school, the queen of the junior prom began showing an interest in me. Her name was Sandy. I remember being flattered, and I welcomed her subtle advances. I began seeing her at the Friday night dances. My sister had taught me the jitterbug, and I was comfortable stepping out in that direction with Sandy at the dances, but that always led to the slow dances near the end of the evening. She allowed me to hold her close, and my feelings were aroused. She was seventeen, and I must say, full-figured. We would kiss and say goodnight as our parents were waiting to pick us up after the dances.

I went home week after week wanting to stay with her somehow, but knowing that was just impossible. I wanted to kiss her more every time, and I think she wanted the same. It would be many months before we were able to arrange a date that allowed us to be alone to cuddle and pet. Our common innocence created a block to our experiments, and our frustration levels rocketed. I believe this is when I fell in love with love. Lacking experience, there was no way for me to know how to take the next step, and there was no way for me to know what to do about it at the time.

My schoolwork was average, except for the math classes I loved. My goals were unknown, except I wanted badly to grow up fast and experience whatever the man in me wanted. I knew where I wanted to go, but I just didn't know how to get there.

I was too young to go out on my own, but when I turned seventeen, I found out with my parents' written permission I could join the army. I gathered all the information and began working on my parents long before my birthday. I came up with an answer for everything, including continuing my education in-service, getting trained in the general area I preferred, and being able to support myself.

After all, the pay was almost $100 each month with all living expenses paid. I would be able to grow up and learn all I should know. Real life awaited me now.

To further set the stage, let me mention that I began life in a small city of Pittsfield, Massachusetts, and my family moved shortly after to the northern suburb of Lanesborough where my father and mother had bought their first home from my paternal grandparents. It was a hilltop cottage at the end of a half-mile street bordering a large area of woods and next door to my grandparents' newly built home. It was a great, yet quiet, place to begin exploring life. My memories begin when I was about five years old living with my parents and my only sister Judy. She was our parents' little helper with me being the new little guy in the family, and it would take a few years for me to wiggle out from under the older sister issues, that after all, were minor issues. Judy had appointed herself as an extra parent, and I felt out-ruled and out-maneuvered. I did not respond well to constant supervision from anyone, let alone my sister.

My grandparents were encouraging and kind. They were old-fashioned to a fault, but warm and loving to me. Both were early risers like I was, and I would visit and have breakfast with them often. My grandfather played the violin and my grandmother was expert on the piano and organ. Neither one of them could sing but no one had told them, so they always sang along. It was kind of funny, but they really did not have a clue. The important thing was that they made me feel special and they were the best of next-door neighbors for many years.

We moved back to Pittsfield into a newly built three-bedroom ranch more suitable for our family when I was fifteen years old, another turning point I would not recognize for many years. My father was an energetic and friendly supervisor at the local GE company, and he proved his family values were outstanding. Having completed only high school level studies and a short tour in the navy in Guam, he took advantage of the business courses offered by his company to advance himself. By the end of his career, cut short by heart problems, we found he was well liked by his employees and co-workers numbering in the hundreds. He had reached the top of his field in that company and retired as the manager of production control for the Ordnance Department. They produced the MPQ4, a mortar locater device for the services that would identify where hostile fire was coming from in combat. He enjoyed the outdoors, fishing of various types, hunting small game, and watching horse races at a nearby track. He would often take me along on the hunting and fishing adventures, which delighted me. He was financially responsible all of his life, even with the added burden of extraordinary medical expenses for my mother, a trait that would elude me for most of my life. My mother was also a high school graduate. She had worked as a restaurant server and as a secretary before she learned she had multiple sclerosis. She gradually became physically disabled, starting when I was around eight years old.

Judy and I would help her with day-to-day chores around the house and with her personal needs. My father learned some physical therapy to aid in her treatment plan and to help her cope with this exhausting disease while also managing the rest of her personal needs. He assumed the shopping and cooking duties while still finding time to study for his work advancements. I am proud of them both and still hear glowing comments about them thirty years after their passing.

Judy and I grew closer when I was about thirteen years old, when we shared information about school and friends. We had accepted our mother as she was. I believe we benefited from these special circumstances and the life lessons learned in our youth, rather than having the feeling we had been shortchanged in someway. Our mother was bright, loving, and humorous. We got along famously while helping her cope with her illness, inabilities, and the pain associated with multiple sclerosis. Her physical limits would increase gradually over twenty-five years until her death at the age of 53. Family members remember my mother's sense of humor even today.

To continue, on the morning of April 17, 1961, my seventeenth birthday, I reported to the office of the local army recruiter with my parents' letter of approval. He drove me to Springfield, Massachusetts's army headquarters, where I finished my paperwork and joined a few other volunteers in taking the oath. I signed up for a three-year hitch with training guaranteed in the administration area of which finance would be a part, if I were lucky enough to get what I actually wanted. We were directed to Fort Dix, New Jersey, for basic combat training.

Two months later, I was reassigned to Fort Benjamin Harrison, Indianapolis, Indiana, for a five week course for postal clerks, also a part of administration, but tedious to a fault. During the first month of this basic period, my life was restricted and in lock step with a company of trainees who were stripped of any impression that they knew anything, or could properly do anything, without doing it in unison, *the army way*. We grew into good physical shape against all odds while learning the basic combat skills intended to save our collective ass in combat.

Camouflage, rifles, bayonets, first aid, and hand grenades occupied all of our waking hours, plus physical training, running long distances loaded down with equipment, and marching until we were ready to fall over.

During the fifth week of basic training, we were rewarded with a day pass on the weekend to go to town and look around. The drinking age was eighteen unless you were wearing a uniform in New Jersey or Indiana, but whatever the case, I did not have to prove my age. My whole life was about to change as I discovered the next true love of my life, alcohol. I immediately noticed the aches and pains of training subsided and my social concerns were gone. I was taller, older, stronger, wiser, bolder, and ready to tackle anything or anyone. I liked the taste of beer and other drinks, but it didn't matter much because I was in search of the effects, not the taste. I wanted all the promises that alcohol offered to me through its enticement. I thought I had finally arrived in life and I was complete. What more could a shy kid ask for? Euphoria warmed my insides and calmed my fears. My life was going to be good, and all these feelings justified my decisions until this day.

The magnetism of the effects of alcohol on my being would then slowly and surely begin to take over my life and my life decisions. This, I would later learn, was an explanation of the expression, "The man takes a drink, the drink takes a drink, and the drink takes the man." My parents and my grandfather all drank and smoked daily and had never displayed any life problems that I knew about. I thought these behaviors were natural, and now feeling it for me, I understood their habits. I did not recognize that the quantities and frequencies of my indulgences would deliver far different results in my lifetime.

I would learn that after exactly four months in the service I would be sent to La Rochelle, France, to work in the Army Post Office. Most of my peers had drawn assignments in either Korea or Germany, where there was more unrest, so I was happy to be going to France, after learning how to cope with everything important in my life by drinking.

The trip by troopship to France was eight days long, crowded, and boring. There was no drinking allowed on board, and I was not aware of any hidden supply. The pounding waves in the Atlantic Ocean in the fall of 1961 would toss and turn the ship on its course to the port in Bremerhaven, Germany. Once on land, we boarded trains headed for our individual destinations in the countries we were assigned to. The sights and sounds of France were mellow and inviting, while I began to adjust to the different architecture and the narrow street designs with sidewalks everywhere for the many people who chose walking and biking over cars. The American army trucks were wide and took up most of the road as we continued from the train station to our new base. The mission of this base was to support the military build-up in Germany by shipping the supplies needed by the advance army contingents to be ready if hostilities began in the Berlin Build-Up.

My mission was to find the Enlisted Men's Club and quickly drink enough beer to settle the turmoil in my mind and in my gut. The warmth and soothing feelings of the alcohol settled me down and made me feel good inside my own skin again. This wasn't going to be that bad after all. I had $100 a month to spend on 25-cent beer, personal items, and, of course, gambling. It took me a little over a week to find out I would have to stop drinking for most of the month because I was running out of money. So I had to become a little more creative financially. I used gambling, borrowing, and taking money from my post office drawer, always thinking I could easily repay any of my losses. I was constantly scheming between those three to cover my debts while providing myself with enough money to drink the way I wanted to drink, and when I wanted to drink. There was a much older specialist named Stonewall Jackson that I worked with in the post office that understood where I was coming from. He therefore continued to lend me money into the hundreds as the months rolled on. By the way, hundreds of dollars in 1961 and '62 were equal to thousands in cash value today.

My need to engage in all of my bad habits was inescapable. I was addicted to all without understanding what addiction was. I had become my own person by the way I *wanted* to live each day without regard to future consequences. Until this time, I had never had to pay any substantial penalties. I felt invincible.

I was also easily distracted by the many young ladies I saw both on base and when I would get the chance to go to town. The age of innocence in France was long gone. The way they looked at sexuality and relationships were decades ahead of the United States. As a seventeen-year-old "boy" plucked from the states and dropped into France, I was wildly anxious to explore my own sexuality. Problem was, I brought all of my other addictions along with me as I began to grow into a "man" carousing the landscape of this exciting land. My day-to-day decisions were greatly influenced by alcohol. My strength and youth gave me the energy to overdo everything.

Chapter 2

Drinking Begins to
Overshadow My Life

During my two years in France and a month in Germany, I began to experience negative outcomes resulting from my frequent drinking and the inability to control my behavior after I started drinking on any given occasion.

The effects alcohol had on me dictated my decisions that always favored continued drinking instead of responsible thinking. I would repeatedly ignore the rules when I was due to return to my company. I often found myself being punished by decrease in rank, or having to perform extra duty after hours, seemingly designed to add control to my life. One drink would make me forget these lessons.

Soon, my pressing money issues would cause me to reenlist in the army for a period of six years, in order to collect the bonus of $600 to pay my debts, all a result of my bad habits. At this time I was able to request reassignment away from the post office position. I was transferred to the Special Services Unit to work at the Bachelor Officer Quarters, located on the other side of Orleans away from the base camp. I became the assistant manager of the BOQ under a Specialist Five, Jerry O'Hara, who drank exactly like I did. We occupied one of the small apartments within the men's BOQ and supervised the female unit from across the courtyard. Transportation was provided by a Special Services taxi service for the lower ranked officers and us, but we would easily be overruled by a senior officer during normal business hours if they needed to go somewhere. Getting a ride when needed would make getting enough beer and occasional food supplies difficult to schedule. My fondest memory of the early months of working and living there was when Jerry returned from the store carrying two loaves of bread on top of two cases of beer. As he made his way down the corridor, he passed the senior officer in charge of the quarters. I could see him grimace, until the colonel called out, "O'Hara!"

Jerry froze and turned to face the officer. The colonel asked, "O'Hara, what in the hell are you going to do with all that bread?"

We all laughed and continued on our way. My work there would soon suffer from my drinking, and I was transferred back to the base on the other side of town to perform menial clerical work in the supply office. I missed drinking with Jerry, and soon after this transfer, I caught a ride to visit him and his supply of beer on a weekend afternoon. We drank until the taxi service ended, and I was forced to walk all the way back to base, blasted from the long afternoon of drinking. It was dark by the time I reached the city between the BOQ and the base, and I was having trouble walking/staggering along the road.

With no logical explanation, I noticed the keys in a small French car parked in the roadway and decided I needed that car to get back to base because I was too drunk to walk. I got in, started the car easily, and headed in the opposite direction, back to the BOQ instead of my base. After several more beers with Jerry, I started driving back to town, finally heading to my base. In the center of town, the car ran out of gas but I resolved to restart it anyway and sat there grinding the engine, waiting for it to start. This drew the attention of a few French citizens, who approached to help me only to find a drunk American who couldn't communicate in the French car. I tried to walk away but was apprehended by the police for stealing the car and being "drunk in public." Let me tell anyone who travels: If you are thinking about getting into trouble in a foreign country, France is not a good idea! When they say, "You are going to prison for two months," they mean sixty-one days, and they mean prison, not a jail.

I was unceremoniously dropped off at the "Maison d'Arret," or house of the arrested. The small cement cubicles were furnished with insect-infested straw mattresses about three inches thick, and there was a pail that would be emptied once a day for anything that may have to come out of my body for the next sixty-one days. I was given a small amount of bread each day with what looked like the broth from someone else's soup. Each day I was allowed to go outside in a high walled pen to exercise for one hour and was allowed a cold shower once each week. My closest cell mate was doing life for killing his mother, and he had the privilege of sewing soccer balls together with his bare hands. He was the only other prisoner who spoke English and French.

After the sixty-one days in prison, and paying the $6.40 fine for being drunk in public, I was released to the Military Police and taken back to my company. The next few hours were spent debriefing and photographing my body. I was then returned to my quarters to bathe and get clean clothes to replace the clothes that I had been wearing the entire time I was in prison. A good description of me would be that of skin and bones, weak and ashen appearance, and covered with insect bites and scabs. All I could think of was getting a drink at the Enlisted Men's Club. And so, my recovery from this event began the same way the adventure had started: by drinking. Everyone thought that they were helping me that day by buying beers for me and listening to my tales of woe while I again drank myself into a state near unconsciousness. I had no clue that alcohol was ruling my life and that I would continue heavily drinking until I took a leave of absence to return to the U.S. in order to marry my sweetheart Sandy.

Remember the queen of the junior prom? What a prize she was getting! I controlled my drinking while on leave to get married and honeymoon on Cape Cod, before getting out of town again to drink the way I wanted. I then returned to France and Germany for a few months before being reassigned to Fort Leonard Wood, Missouri.

When I was allowed to return to the U.S., I collected my new wife in Massachusetts after another eight days at sea and took a bus to Fort Leonard Wood. This time I had found the secreted supply of rum for $6 per bottle, and the trip seemed quicker and absent of any concerns about being seasick. No one noticed my staggering. They all thought it was the ship. Specialist Four was the rank I had been promoted to by this time, and I was not assigned on-base quarters for my family because of my rank and having less than four years in the service. Sandy and I found a trailer for rent off post and we settled in.

My job assignment was in personnel processing at the base. There, I interviewed new men coming into the army for placement and training recommendations. Work went well in the early months, and I was promoted to Specialist Five. Sandy and I would learn that she was expecting our first child exactly nine months after my return to the States. Shortly before that event, we were assigned a nice duplex on post and enjoyed living there. It was like new. My drinking was on the increase, and little spats erupted from time to time concerning the frequency and amount of my drinking. Sandy was not happy, and she took her first opportunity to visit her parents in Massachusetts after Kimberly Jean was born on July 30, 1964. She returned home after a few weeks only to find that I had been drinking uncontrollably since she had left. We argued at length, and I promised to cut down on the drinking to please her. Having been promoted to staff sergeant, I was then responsible for the overseas levy process for the personnel permanently assigned to Fort Leonard Wood.

After I became a father, I altered my course somewhat because of my added responsibilities at home. I was proud of my family, but drinking was an active part of my three years in Missouri. I was often challenged about my drinking. I then prepared a plan to volunteer to serve in Vietnam, where I might get a promotion, and, more importantly, get away from the drinking controls Sandy was trying to place on me. This was a drastic way to correct my position, and made no sense at all when you consider that I would end up in combat in Vietnam as a result. My alcoholic thinking had found a temporary solution without any foresight into what impact a one-year tour of duty in combat would have on me. Moreover, it was a mindless decision that would alter my life forever.

I made the arrangements for my wife and daughter to return home to Massachusetts in December 1966, where I vacationed for a few weeks. I flew to San Francisco the first week of January 1967 in order to proceed to my flight to Vietnam. I was pretty well blasted when I boarded the plane and slept for a long while as the flight began. Well into the flight, I introduced myself to a fellow staff sergeant, who had also been assigned to a unit of the 25th Infantry Division located in Cu Chi where I, too, was headed. His particular assignment was much different than mine, as he was an infantry platoon leader, and I was a personnel sergeant headed for the Division Headquarters unit. There, I would take over the job of the NCOIC (non-commissioned officer in charge) of the casualty-reporting branch.

Visiting with him for over 12 hours would prove to be a turning point in my life.

Jerry L. Spicer was a seasoned staff sergeant with years of experience in leading infantrymen in combat. I had only five years and nine months in the service and no combat experience, so I was all ears on the flight into Vietnam. We quickly made friends because we both had young daughters we loved to talk about whenever it could be squeezed in. Jerry was an openly friendly type of guy who welcomed the chance to help me with the experience he possessed. A calm and reassuring voice was welcomed on the flight into combat. My nerves were tightening the closer we got to Vietnam, and I began to realize what I didn't know.

After landing with armed guards surrounding the plane, we disembarked into the one hundred-plus degree heat of the night and were rushed to the cover of a building used to further process the incoming troops. It was here that I was offered the opportunity to stay in Saigon headquarters to work by the personnel manager because they were short on personnel and appeared to like me. For months, I had been talking about the history of the 25th Infantry Division that I had originally been assigned to, so I passed on the opportunity and continued to Cu Chi with Jerry still with me. It was really cool to have a friend beside me because I was nervous about everything that now surrounded me. The sights, the smells of burning diesel fuel and Agent Orange spray, the constant smell of waste material, and the strange noises of an active war were unknown and shocking to my system.

It was so hot and humid that I could hardly breathe. A deep fear began to grow in me like a knot in my stomach. The trip to Cu Chi in the back of large open trucks in convoy escorted by heavily armed helicopters in the early hours of the day was scary, but I was reassured because I was near my new friend Jerry. We arrived at the division camp located in a clearing in the middle of the Iron Triangle, which was jungle area filled with enemy tunnels about twenty miles northwest of Saigon. I settled into a small, tent like, partially wooden building that was built a few feet off the ground because of the monsoon seasons that constantly flooded everything. Each building had an attached sandbagged bunker to afford cover during mortar and recoilless rifle round attacks. I would quickly learn that this would be an everyday event. My work tent was a few hundred yards away from the headquarters, and I was soon to learn that much of my actual work would be to gather casualty information from the hospital or the medical evacuation areas located about the camp. The morbid reality of casualty counts kept me in a state of nervous melancholy.

The constant din, however, of rounds fired by our defensive artillery and the disrupted air just a few feet above my head, provided an odd but effective distraction. These rounds were fired from the area to which Jerry was initially assigned, but he was sent out to the field to join his platoon shortly after arriving.

It did not take me long to find the NCO (non-commissioned officer) club building, where coolers were always stocked with Budweiser cans. I knew that alcohol would calm my nerves and overshadow the fears that were trying to burst from deep within me, but I had to control myself in order to perform my duties. The balancing act had begun. Can I drink now? Should I stop drinking now? Will anyone notice me? Will I be able to sleep for a while to escape my fears for part of the night?

Within a few weeks of my new assignment, I was at the helicopter pad of a clinic when I was asked to help carry litters containing wounded men to the doctors and nurses inside their building for emergency treatment. There had been an increased number of casualties that day because of a new fight near our camp, and the medical evacuation choppers were constantly landing with more and more casualties. A mine had hit the soldier I first helped to carry in, partially severing both of his legs and one of his arms, along with causing some head injuries from the shrapnel. His pain was obviously excruciating, and it took four of us to hold him down while the doctors tried to stop the bleeding and help his pain. I tried to look away, as I was not trained or experienced in working with emergency patients. In the heat of the moment, I had not recognized Jerry, my newly found friend, but I did some twenty minutes later when his pain suddenly stopped. The arm I was holding down went limp, and so did I. He was finally dead. My legs were weak, but I stumbled to the rear of the building where I had to sit on the ground to cry, propped up against the back of the Emergency Room building. I was in shock.

My thinking was in slow motion, my reality out of focus. Was this really Jerry?

How could this have happened to him? Why did he have to die? My thinking had begun to circle around and around. I was nauseous, not able to concentrate. My job was the last thing on my mind. War was personal now.

Someone grabbed me by the shoulder and pulled me up to return to the heliport to carry more of the wounded. By now the body bags were gathering just off the pad, as not all who were coming in were in time to be helped. My buddy

Jerry had been placed in a thick, black rubber body bag and put there as well, just before the Chaplain moved from bag to bag praying for those lost, giving them last rites. I will never forget his tears marking each black bag as he prayed over them, one by one. The vicious lethal wounds he had to experience in order to perform his duties as Chaplain challenged the innocence of that gentle man. It has always made me wonder how deep the Chaplain's wounds are, even today, if he's still alive and not trapped within his own mind. I know that he had prayed with them every day and loved them like they were a living part of his own family, God's family. The Chaplain's grief was overwhelming; he couldn't talk to anyone. I don't even remember him leaving the area; he just wasn't there anymore. I never knew his name, and I cannot remember his face. I just remember him bending over each body, crying, praying. And then he was gone.

My official duty was to gather information about the wounds, time, place, and nature of the action where the casualties had occurred. I pressed forward beyond my personal upset but felt numb and distracted. Later, I would realize that I found it impossible to complete the one report I knew the best. I continued breaking down emotionally time and time again. Someone else would have to draft the letter to the next of kin for Staff Sergeant Jerry Spicer. I was unable to compose such a draft on that day, and for several years to follow I could not commit anything about these events to paper. These experiences would swirl around and around in my head anytime I tried to rest. The radio static and voices, the sounds of the chopper, the dust being blown everywhere as the choppers set down, the urgency, the inner fear, heat, sweat, blood, and the color of death. This story has never ended. It just kept replaying in my mind, and it never changed. My brain cells were permanently scarred with these memories, and recovery from that did not seem to be an option. Drinking helped me cope, or so I thought.

My letter entitled, "Dear Miss Jamie," would be published in the newspaper of my local community college, which I was attending part-time around 1971. It was a story about my experience in Vietnam that focused on Sergeant Spicer, and it was never sent to his family. I walked away from the college, that town, and my family shortly after my story was published. I had arrived at the title because my memory incorrectly recalled Jerry's daughter's name, which is actually Cindy. She also had an older brother named Steve who never made it into my dreams. I have also learned that Cindy was a few years older than my daughter Kimberly Jean.

My memory of some of the details through a long series of nightmares that followed me for many years had distorted some of the facts. It was unpopular to talk or write about Vietnam in that era, and it was better left unsaid, but I needed to write and feel again, to help me past the nightmares.

The college weekly paper was the only media where I could express some of my thoughts and feelings. The events of that one day in Vietnam would replay night after night in my dreams for years, gripping me in depression fueled by alcohol.

The torments of war run deeper than most people know and affected many of us who made it out of Vietnam alive, but were damaged in ways other than physical.

There is a bumper sticker that says, "Over medicated for your protection."

Veterans, suffering from PTSD, must have authored this informative blurb, and it is only those unfamiliar with combat who read it with humor. Decades of treatment follow these men and women with little understanding from the outside world. I have always held those who were heroes in the highest esteem. I then, and still, question whether or not I possess the qualities necessary to respond instead of react to danger. I am moved by many stories that came out of combat, and I was greatly affected by what I learned from those who witnessed the action resulting in my friend's death. Apparently, his platoon was pinned down and one of his men was lying in the open, needing help after being hit by enemy fire. Jerry disregarded his own safety and tried to get to his men to assist their wounded comrade. In the ensuing chaos, Jerry stepped on a land mine, becoming another casualty of the war. "Dust Off Five" landed in the middle of this mess to pick him up, creating another layer of heroism by their acts.

"He continued to direct his platoon until he was forcibly evacuated," is stated in one of the two Bronze Star Metals for Heroism citations that he earned that day, posthumously. "Sergeant Spicer, because of his loyalty to his men and strong devotion to duty, sacrificed his life in order to save his fellow soldiers. Sergeant Spicer's loyalty to his comrades and his complete disregard for personal safety in the face of danger reflect great credit upon himself, his unit, and the United States Army." This citation was signed by the Commander of the United States Army in Vietnam by the direction of the President of the United States under the provisions of Executive Order 11046, and dated 24 August 1967 for the date of action: 3 February 1967 in the Republic of Vietnam.

A copy of that citation is on my wall of memories along with Jerry's picture that appeared in the newspaper shortly after his sacrifice. You cannot give more than that to your country and your fellow man. I lost a friend of about a month, our country lost the most courageous hero I ever knew, and his family lost everything.

Cindy and Steve Spicer would have to grow up without their guiding light.

It pains me to realize that millions of people would never know of Sergeant Spicer's commitment to our liberty, except that his name now appears on the Vietnam Wall Monument. One of over 58,000 names. One of over 58,000 stories.

Most Americans have tried to forget Vietnam for their own reasons, while some of us have to remember because of our experience. In my opinion, to let their memories be forgotten would take away their heroism and the meaning of the lives they gave for us. Also lost would be the sacrifices of all the family members who were left to feel the terrible pains of loss. "Support our troops" is a simple phrase, however inbred with great meaning to those who served. Trading places with them, if you could, would mean that you would have been dead for the last forty-plus years. That is how much life they have missed so far, on a selfless mission to protect our rights and serve our country.

The rest of my year in Vietnam was spent in constant fear, anesthetized by alcohol as often as possible. For the last five months of service, I was transferred to a camp called Dong Tam in the Mekong Delta, where I was assigned as the personnel staff non-commissioned officer for the 3rdSurgical Hospital (MASH). As the name implies, it was a mobile army surgical hospital. It was erected by inflating rubber buildings to house the hospital equipment in climate-controlled air and rooms to operate, in support of combat operations in the area. A large staff of medical professionals manned the hospital.

This assignment for me was tantamount to respite, for following my experiences in Cu Chi reporting casualties for seven months, I was non-productive mentally. I tried to drink beer as often and as long as I could. I passed out at the end of each day, in order to get through the nights filled with the sounds of incoming and outgoing munitions. Others were wounded and even killed nearby as I slept, but I remained physically unscathed, ending my one-year tour in the last week of December 1967. I returned to the States, got a bath and a fresh dress uniform for travel, and flew to Massachusetts, putting Vietnam and combat behind me. Or so I thought.

My wife Sandy and daughter moved to Fort Meade, Maryland, to my next and final assignment in the army. That spring, I was diagnosed with manic-depressive psychosis and was treated at Walter Reed Army Hospital for sixty-one days in a locked ward. I experienced unexplainable high and low extremes of my emotions and was acting erratically, causing my wife to refer me for help at the local clinic, who then transferred me to Walter Reed for "three days of observation." Shortly after arriving at the hospital, I experienced a complete emotional breakdown and was heavily sedated with Thorazine for a long time while the medics tried to work with me. Their diagnosis was based on my current behavior, rather than looking into what I had endured in Vietnam just months earlier that may have set up the mood swings I was experiencing. I do not believe that post-traumatic stress disorder, or PTSD, was identified in early 1968. Most of my time was spent moving about in a "Thorazine Shuffle" because the heavy medication only allowed me to shuffle rather than walk. It also promoted eating and sleeping, constantly!

After my release from the hospital, I returned home and worked only intermittently for the next month or so. My enlisted term of service was ending, and I had no intention of reenlisting for any amount of money, or extending my service, knowing I could not face anything like Vietnam again. I secured a civilian job training in the investment field near the end of my service, schooling myself for a securities test to begin selling stocks and mutual funds for a company in the District of Columbia when discharged from the army in August 1968.

After several lackluster months within the D.C. company, my father-in-law, back in Pittsfield, Massachusetts, convinced me to move back home and restart my career in a local securities firm where he had influence.

More training was offered to further qualify on the New York Stock Exchange, and again I started slowly to begin work to develop a clientèle to support my family. Having my wife and daughter close to our permanent home again made everyone happy, except for my wife. She announced she was pregnant with our second child. Our marriage began to unravel for the next year and a half, in part due to my drinking and lack of substantial success selling stocks for the new company. I was forced out of my home, informed I was separated, and divorced. My job was in jeopardy. This was due to a declining market, and impending consolidation at all brokerage firms during that era. This impacted me first, as I was the lowest of the brokers in my office who also, coincidently, appeared to have a drinking problem.

I then traveled to Maine with some friends, where I found an opportunity to work in the timber industry at an entry-level wood yard job cutting trees into various log lengths. The obvious change to brute physical labor was surprisingly rewarding to me, as I built up my physical strength, stamina, and eating capacities. My drinking increased but appeared to have less of an impact on me overall. After six months at this job, I returned to Massachusetts and found work as a cook in the restaurant/motel where I was temporarily living.

Soon after, I worked in a mill grinding aircraft parts, while developing a relationship with my second wife, Nancy. She was a clerk at the local state employment office and a part-time bartender (a job I enjoyed watching her do). A few years after our marriage, my drinking challenged that relationship. I moved to a nearby town in order to continue to drink the way I wanted to. I found a job working on a road crew that cleared trees away from power lines. My drinking increased greatly, and I was physically and mentally a mess.

A co-worker/friend (and apparently a member of Alcoholics Anonymous) suggested I try to get help at the Albany New York Veterans Hospital rehabilitation unit, which was only about sixty miles away from where I lived. Not having any solutions of my own, I agreed to take his advice, not knowing what was in store for me. My life had evolved into a circle of drinking to live and living to drink, while my mind played tricks on me. The effects of alcohol guided all my decisions. There was not much left for me to do. He put me, my suitcase, and a six-pack of beer in the back of his van, and we were off.

I would be diagnosed and treated for alcoholism (which was bloody obvious) and post-traumatic stress disorder. PTSD was probably a more definitive or evolving diagnosis for manic depressive as a result of treatment and the passage of time. The five-week PTSD program was excellent for me, and was followed with Alcoholism Rehabilitation for another four weeks in the same facility in late 1977.

During the following year after treatment, I worked as the cook and then the director of a halfway house where I lived in Albany, New York, which was called the St. Peter's Rehabilitation Center. Father Peter Young, a strong and noted advocate for rehabilitation, opened the halfway house. I found my way into many different AA meetings around the Capitol District, and into a new job selling insurance for a fraternal organization. One year into my newfound sobriety, I married my third wife Stacey, who was also a member of AA (Nancy had divorced me while I was in the hospital a year earlier).

Three-and-a-half years later, while working out of town, I somehow decided I could drink safely again because no one would know. No one except Stacey, who immediately chose sobriety over a marriage to an active drunk. She dutifully arranged for an AA intervention to try to help me, but I could no longer choose not to drink. This event would signal the start of many years of coming and going from rehabilitation centers to AA meetings, to continued attempts to drink safely again, while challenging fate along the way. Progression was wearing me down. The more times I tried to drink, the quicker it would be for the effects of my drinking to interfere with my life. Once I began to drink, I could not control how long or how much I would drink. My resistance to the effects of alcohol was gradually disappearing.

It would take sobriety a while to catch up with me, but it finally did. The key to the start of meaningful recovery for me had been to attack both problems that were affecting me the most at the same time. Whatever makes your life unmanageable needs to be addressed. Of course, the serious introduction to the tenets of AA was the ultimate solution in my life. I would constantly find my way back to AA when my world turned to crap because of my drinking. Deep inside, I had learned there was a way out, and I was always welcomed to try again. That knowledge ultimately saved my life. With sobriety on my side, I was able to address any other issue that caused me problems.

Alcoholics Anonymous gets the final credit for my sobriety, as they were the ones to show me the way that would work over time. How I lived through all those ups and downs, the over medications, the serious thoughts of drunken suicide, and the inherent dangers of addiction before I got to the AA rooms is truly unknown.

Something greater than I was definitely at the controls of my life. Learning more about the process suggested by AA was the way that I began to grow spiritually, while learning a way of life that was not counterproductive. I believe that most alcoholics are extremely repetitious types of people, and once they begin an acceptable manner of living they find it easier and easier to stay sober as time goes by, and their rewards of sobriety have a chance to impact their lives. In the car business, the old expression would be, "If it ain't broke, don't fix it!" AA works just the way it was originally formatted and practiced for over seven decades. You can rely on all of their books and teachings. The local fellowships give voice and encouragement with love to those who need our help. We cannot maintain our own sobriety without giving it away as freely as we received it. AA will always be there.

CHAPTER 3

Sobriety is the Foundation, Not the Cure

I could not have begun my journey "on borrowed time" without sobriety, which started with meaningful intervention, several attempts at rehabilitation, many life failures, and the gradual acceptance of the famous twelve-step program. It took about ten years for the program to overtake my insanity. For a long time, I could have been called a periodic alcoholic rather than a daily drunk, and I was absolutely cunning about planning my next drink. That probably accounts for my protracted recovery and pain. I wasn't fooling others in the program, but I was good at fooling myself. I am sure they were just waiting for me to come out of the fog. Being a periodic alcoholic simply means there are periods of dryness between drinking times overshadowed by the inability to predict the outcome and the problems when drinking is resumed.

The progression of alcoholism is not delayed or improved by one or more periods of abstinence. The downward spiral continues, even without drinking. *I could not win until I surrendered!* One must honestly admit dependency and admit that their lives have become unmanageable before a forward step can be taken, or the perils too numerous to describe await anyone with a drinking problem who fails to stay sober. There are many ways to get drunk and really only one way to get sober.

If someone has reached this critical point of concern about their life and their drinking, progression in the disease is displayed, and cannot be denied safely.

Many stronger and wiser men have tried to find an easier softer way, but they could not, "until we let go absolutely," something of note in the fifth chapter of AA.

As I was approaching my commitment to marry my fourth wife Betty, I had finally resolved to surrender to my alcoholism with Betty's encouragement. I wanted to succeed in marriage (finally) and in life. I knew it was going to have to be without alcohol. September 5, 1993, the day we married, would become my sobriety date, and life appeared to normalize as if on cue. I felt better, ate better, worked more productively, and my memory began to be restored, which helped everything. Sobriety doesn't automatically solve all of life's problems, but it does lay the foundation for understanding, growth, and improvement.

Our marriage was meaningful and complete, my job more manageable, and my relationships with friends and family were deep and rewarding, replacing the self-isolation caused by my alcoholism. Betty and I had found a perfect piece of property in rural Melrose, New York, just ten miles from my work. We cleared part of the land and built a lovely large ranch-styled home on our hillside. It was beautiful, a place I could see myself spending the rest of my life in. The sights and smells of the country were relaxing. Life was going well in my recovery.

In the summer of 1998, I was working as an automobile salesman and manager with fifteen years of reasonable success in this field. I felt that I was well liked by both my customers and my peers, and I was enjoying a good life with a great family. For about a week, I had often felt dizzy and tired, which was unfamiliar to me. I went home not feeling well twice in one day. I had a stressful meeting scheduled during the evening hours I wanted to attend. I started to have chest pains, cold sweats, and I felt pressure in my upper torso. The symptoms quieted between trips to the office, but became worse by the minute when I had finally returned to my home later that day. Betty and I had no experience with heart attacks, so we were about to embark on a new and scary path of our lives together.

After calling the rescue squad, the ambulance attendants stuffed nitroglycerin under my tongue, started an IV, and hooked up oxygen to help my symptoms, all while monitoring my vital signs. I was carried out doors, down the steep embankment in front of my home, and transported to the nearest hospital, about seven miles away. The ambulance did not immediately get underway because the nurses did not feel I was yet stable enough to transport. I listened to the open radio communication between the attendants and the emergency-room doctor who was supervising from the hospital. The memories from that day in Vietnam rushed into my head. The rescue squad was dressed in combat fatigues from the Army National Guard, who were in the area responding to a recent tornado in a nearby community. I felt that I was back in Vietnam, and it was my turn now.

I really had not understood at this point that I was in fact close to death. Once at the emergency room, I could see that the attending doctors and nurses were not comfortable about treating me, as they were not normally a cardiac provider, nor did they have a specialist available to treat me in the emergency room when I arrived. The nurses were reading the instructions. An on-call doctor, R. Scott Morris, arrived and stabilized me after an hour had passed. He ordered a second ambulance to transfer me to another hospital ten miles away, where his cardiology associate would have the technical support and personnel needed to operate on me.

On arrival at this hospital, I was rolled at once into the catheterization lab, where a full medical staff awaited me. My new hero, Dr. Louis Papandrea, was all about getting started. He quickly explained he was going to perform an angioplasty and try to correct the blockage that was causing the pain and the unbearable pressure. After opening my blocked right coronary artery, he implanted a metal stent to reinforce the damaged wall of the artery, allowing the blood to flow again. The lower portion of my heart had been cut off from a good flow of oxygenated blood for so long that much of the area was now dead. That circumstance predicted life with some restrictions and some pain, but I cheerfully accepted this since the alternative sucked. A few days in the hospital, a few weeks at home in recovery, and the start of a new cardiac rehabilitation program would put me on the path of return to work. I was told to stop smoking, but was only able to cut down, which demonstrates addiction to be a tree that can have several branches.

My downtime gave me reason to ponder what had happened to me, and what it all meant at the end of the day. Belatedly, I began thinking about what might have happened if I had not successfully stopped drinking some time before this first medical emergency. Like anyone who medicates themselves with their drug of choice, I would not have been aware of the urgency of my symptoms, because they would have been fogged over, or I could have been in a blackout, or just plain unconscious. The knee-jerk reaction of any addict to pain is to medicate, which in this circumstance would have resulted in death rather than recovery. By this example, I began to appreciate where I finally arrived in life, and was anxious to return to work to build upon my successes. I believed I was still alive for some special reason that was unclear to me. As my life unfolds today, I have begun to see glimmers of new and better events in my life. The search goes on.

The months slipped by as I adjusted to my new restrictions of life habits, diet, multiple medications, and cardiac exercise. Routine follow-up visits with doctors brought a series of medication adjustments, depending on how I was feeling and, of course, the doctor's observations, experience, and various test results along the way. Most everything seemed to be under control, until one fateful Saturday morning at work, eleven months after the stent had been implanted in my right coronary artery.

While in my office, I suddenly had extreme pain and pressure in my chest and was experiencing hot feelings in my head and neck. My left arm also hurt. I asked a co-worker to call an ambulance while I started nitroglycerin treatments every few minutes. All the signs of another major heart attack were present, and the rescue team worked fast to get me ready to transport to the hospital, three miles away. My co-workers showed great concern and helped move furniture out of my office to allow the medics room to load me onto the stretcher. I was wheeled out through the showroom to a place under the garage canopy and loaded into the ambulance with many friends looking on. Several of them observed that a bird had landed on my chest just before I was lifted into the ambulance and were left to ponder the meaning of that occurrence. Once again, I was expedited into the catheterization lab to awaiting doctors who quickly learned that my stent had re-closed in my artery, blocking the flow of blood. They proceeded to attempt to reopen the pathway through the stent by using a rotoblade to drill through the blockage. The attending nurse would count ten seconds while the doctor was drilling, and ten seconds of rest in between, because the procedure caused great pain and I was fully awake. The drilling was repeated many times until they succeeded in getting to the other side of the blockage several minutes later. I nearly passed out from the excruciating pain and was exhausted at the end of the procedure. I was then sent to recovery for an hour, and finally back to a regular hospital room in the cardiac ward to rest.

Stents of that era were not foolproof and were known to fail occasionally. One of the benefits of my age was that the heart muscle was inclined to develop collateral arteries around problem spots during one's fifties. That process had started to occur, and luckily, would continue to develop after this operation. Three months later, I would return to the same hospital with chest pain, only to learn that my circumflex artery was nearly blocked and needed a stent implanted.

The right coronary artery was being cared for internally by way of the natural bypass process, and this procedure would signal a quieting of symptoms and immediate problems. As time went on, the stent permanently re-closed and could no longer be repaired, leaving only the collateral arteries to feed the damaged area of my heart.

Four months later, in December 1999, I was walking in the car lot at work smoking one of the few cigarettes I had cut down to, when out of nowhere and with absolutely no warning, I began to vomit bright, red, steaming hot blood. Shock was the only response I can remember. I returned to my office and called my cardiologist about this amazing development and was told the bleeding would have nothing to do with my heart. They suggested I go to the emergency room. While waiting for their response, I had quieted myself and felt better in only a few minutes. I left work and headed home to rest, not understanding anything about these events. On arrival at home some ten miles away, I started to vomit blood again.

Betty drove me to the emergency room, where it was easy to demonstrate what was wrong with me using a handy waste can. I was admitted for tests, beginning with the doctors looking down my throat and taking a sample of tissue from my bronchial tubes or deeper, which looked suspicious to them. The lab test was positive for cancer. I can only explain in layman terms that this cancer had grown to such a size that it had eaten into the veins and arteries leading into my right lung, and had spread into the lung, which had caused me to start to bleed to death.

I was told the only treatment would be an operation to remove the entire right lung, and they would not schedule the operation until after I had been tested in many other areas to make sure the cancer had not already spread to any other area or organs. They admitted no operation would be performed if they found other cancers. Treatment would have been limited to making me comfortable in my final hours.

My oldest daughter, Kimberly Jean, was scheduled to deliver her first child the same day, so we asked to wait a day, not wanting to upset her at a time like this.

The doctors agreed, so long as I remain at rest in the hospital. Betty drove to Massachusetts, where she was able to see my daughter and new granddaughter in person and give her the news about my condition after she had delivered Alyssa Paige. The following morning I was prepared for surgery, and off I went in a drug-induced haze. The decisions were behind me now, and the concerns of heart complications during the surgery were in someone else's hands. I never have trouble remembering Alyssa Paige's birthday, which we now celebrate together in my recovery from cancer.

The surgeon accessed my chest cavity by way of an incision about a foot and a half long through my back. Upon removing all three lobes of my right lung, he discovered suspicious looking lymph nodes and removed twelve of them. Six would prove to be affected by the active cancer.

The surgeon was later quoted as saying that he had "cleaned me out real good!" He was an overtly religious man who refused to take any credit for his work on me. He noted that the surgery would have to be followed up with three to four months of chemotherapy, if I were to be given a chance to survive more than four months. The statistics were against me, with suspicions whirling; the cancer could have easily traveled anywhere by way of the lymph nodes. He had discovered the one thing that would have stopped the surgery had the lymph node involvement been found prior to surgery. More borrowed time.

This had been a serious and radical surgery that lasted over seven hours with many doctors and nurses. I was sedated for ten days while on life support, as I began my initial recovery. During this time, I would experience many scary moments of semi-consciousness, where I would think I was dying. I dreamed of being carried off to a loading dock in the hospital to dispose of me, and other unexplainable, yet very real, nightmares. I was racked with pain all over when they began to allow me to wake up. I could barely move a muscle without crying out. I then realized breathing was a new adventure. Short shallow breaths were all I could manage, and with a lot of pain in the process. I was discouraged and drug-affected for many days to follow. My throat was raw from the operation and I had been in the hospital since the 9th of December.

I was headstrong about getting out of the hospital sooner rather than later, which left me feeling aggravated. Christmas was only a few days away, and going home was all I could think about, primarily because I had not been able to eat the hospital food to save my butt. Had I not been so affected by the heavy drugs colliding with my "drug history" of alcohol abuse, my reasoning would have been totally different.

I pestered the doctors and staff so much that I was released to go home well before the proper time had elapsed. My wife drove me to our home, where my eldest stepson, Patrick, who had to help me up a flight of stairs from the garage to the living room, joined us. I could only crawl along the floor, so he grabbed the back of my belt to lift me and lighten the load, as I slowly crawled up the stairs.

Upon reaching the floor above, I was released to just lie there for a time to rest from the ordeal. Within the hour, I had managed to get myself onto our couch, where many hours and days would be spent thereafter.

These are the times in one's life when you ponder the decisions that encourage recovery from something like this catastrophic disease and operation. The personal cost down the road is not spelled out when the medical staff is trying to persuade you to authorize the operation and all of the treatment that follows. In all honesty, I had not hesitated to approve the operation, but when I look back I have to wonder about the amount of suffering I opened up for myself and others close to me. Is living at all costs the only decision?

For three or four weeks, moving, eating, and breathing were challenging events.

Some medication had followed me home, but with a low tolerance for pain, it never felt like it was strong enough. Mentally, I was "silly putty," and physically, I was still in a lot of pain. Betty endured more trouble and heartache than anyone knows during these times. My friends and relatives were supportive, but remained in the dark as to the effects it was having on Betty. Everyone expects the spouse to stand strong during an illness, but they never calculate their personal cost. Within four weeks, I had been scheduled to begin a regiment of chemotherapy. I was still weak, but made myself ready for the trip to the hospital. This would at least get me out of the house and give Betty a break from having to work as my personal nurse. The process of getting moved to the hospital and back home every day was physically difficult in the early stages of treatment. The treatments themselves would protract my recovery because of the killer drugs that were infused into me. The whole idea was to introduce poison into my system to attack any remaining cancer cells still floating around in my blood stream. The medicine sometimes attacked healthy cells by mistake, creating some confusion for my body.

The treatment schedule was for five hours of IV infusion each day, five days a week, every third week for three to four months, depending on progress noted. I had noticed my insurance was paying $1,700 per day for the treatments and was damn glad to have them on board! My best friend, Billy Osher, helped Betty file the necessary papers so we would get $156 per week while I was disabled from work. That was it!

The infusions were given in a comfortable easy chair with portable medicine carriers so that one could wander to the restroom many times during the treatment, a known by-product of chemotherapy. I would spend most of the time reading or watching mindless TV, while Betty exercised her freedom from *her* "cancer." Unfortunately, her mother had been admitted to another hospital for treatment several weeks earlier. Betty's time was often spent running between hospitals, on the phone updating friends and relatives, and checking up on my daughter with our newborn grandchild. Betty's mom passed away the day after Christmas, a loss made all the more difficult to process considering the poignancy of the season and the considerable burdens she currently shouldered.

The effects of the chemotherapy to my system were numerous. First of all, as intended, the chemotherapy would attack any fast-growing cells in my body, some of which could be cancerous. There are many other fast-growing cells, such as hair and parts of the mouth and tongue, which would be killed as consequence of the friendly fire. All of my taste senses were altered, making eating a new kind of adventure, in addition to hair loss and ruinous digestive concerns. My food of choice was usually canned fruit and juices, as solid food proved indigestible. I lost about fifty pounds in a short time, but leveled off at what can be described as "skeletal" proportions. My inability to exercise contributed to an over-all weakness that prevailed during these times. My appearance was pale and pasty. Twice I was hospitalized for a few days as a direct result of the effects of the chemotherapy but continued to be treated. I was so weak after each infusion cycle that it took the other two weeks in between to recoup my strength to start again.

In late March 2000, the treatments were discontinued, as my tolerance to the drugs was too low. My oncologist thought that given recent test results and examinations, the chemotherapy had done the intended job of killing any re-sidual cancer cells and that it was time to move on. I would have jumped up and down if that were possible.

By mid-April 2000, my thoughts returned to work and earning a living. I set off to my office to try part-time sales, while beginning to gain ground in recovery. One of my lin-gering concerns arose during this period. My throat was al-ways sore, and as I increased my talking (I was a salesman), the pain increased as well. Several days, I found myself going home early because the pain was actually causing me to vomit. I returned to my oncologist, fearing that cancer was causing the pain, but he referred me to a local throat (ENT) doctor.

This doctor concluded that acid reflux was the culprit, and he prescribed medication to address this condition. Several follow-up exams later, and still in pain, I went to my primary-care physician. He then referred me to a throat specialist who worked at the same hospital that handled my cardiology problems and most of my catheterization procedures. His im-mediate response was to suggest an exploratory operation, so he could use larger instruments and lights in order to find out what was causing my extreme and protracted pain. To his surprise, I authorized the procedure immediately, and was admitted that day to have the operation.

It was exactly a year since the big operation, and I needed help with my voice and the pain. The painful raspy sound of my voice was a constant reminder of my concerns and was limiting my effectiveness as a salesman, relying on communication to earn my salary.

During the follow-up visit after the operation, the doctor told me I was stabbed accidentally in the intubation process of my cancer operation, which was not uncommon. I lay there for ten days, a tube impaling my throat. He said that he widened my throat to allow better breathing and swallowing, but that scarring would result in a continued raspy quality to my speech. He was confident that most of the pain would subside in a week or ten days, and he was entirely correct.

Today I still sound like a frog.

After a week of quiet recovery, I was able to return to work and double my efforts at selling and working fifty to sixty hours a week, which is normal for my job. I continued follow-up visits to my oncologist and cardiologist. One morning, in December 2002, when I was getting ready to visit the oncologist, I stepped out of the shower feeling dizzy and light-headed. I quickly sat down on the toilet seat and passed out cold, falling forward, head first, to the cold marble floor in the bathroom. Shortly after, I awoke and got myself up to the sink and mirror. I saw blood flowing from my forehead, which had taken the brunt of my fall. I had no idea what caused this. I prepared to go to the oncology office and relate this to them. They referred me at once to my cardiologist this time, and we were off to their offices straight away.

Upon examination, the cardiologists suspected that ventricular tachycardia had caused me to pass out. They involved an electro cardiologist to evaluate me and design a pacemaker and defibrillator to control and treat future episodes.

Apparently, heart damage from the previous attacks caused residual electrical damage in my heart or arrhythmias that now could spontaneously stop my heart.

These miraculous devices would produce an electrical shock to restart my heart, hopefully at a normal pace. These events were not, and are not, predictable. The implanted cardiac device would have to do the work on demand. Seventeen months later, on the April 8, 2004, I would learn how that shock would feel.

I was getting ready for an appointment with a friend in the automobile business when I began feeling dizzy. I headed toward our living room couch from the kitchen when I was hit with the shock straight to the bottom of my heart. It felt like someone had shot me at point-blank range in the lower center of my chest, and my first reaction was thinking that it was over for me now. In only a few seconds, I realized I was tingling all over from the shock, and the pain quickly subsided. The computer would later indicate eight and a half seconds had elapsed between the onset of the arrhythmia and the delivery of the treatment that slammed me in the chest. I would rest that day and make an appointment to see my electro cardiologist the next day, by instruction.

Dr. Ian Santoro made several adjustments to my device by computer link-up that day and scheduled an in-hospital test of the adjusted cardiac device. With an external defibrillator at the ready, I was anesthetized. He then stimulated an arrhythmia to observe the reaction of my device. The test went well, and I returned to my home later that day. No one ever explained how I was awakened from the event in my bathroom. Apparently, just another day on borrowed time.

It might seem that all these medical events would be enough for one guy, but a few months later I was diagnosed with congestive heart failure, and a different regiment of medications was integrated into my daily life. This condition was aggravated by the heart damage that had accumulated over time. My blood pressure was low because of the heart damage, and some of the medications can exacerbate this problem. Despite the thirteen prescriptions I take every day,

I still have heart and chest pains, in addition to shortness of breath. CHF is not necessarily a short-term problem, but rather it's a long-term prediction. Few treatments or corrections are available, especially for someone with one lung and a history of cancer.

My survivability is in question when further operations are considered. I am careful to follow my instructions, and am so far succeeding in extending my life well beyond expectations.

In December 2006, after twenty-four years in the car business, I finally gave into disability retirement in order to take better care of myself. This would eliminate the negative effects of the weather and stress that were becoming problematic in my daily work life. The physical restrictions were limiting normal production, and my declining value to the company was becoming painfully apparent. It was a big adjustment after leaving an active work routine, but I settled into retirement out of necessity.

If history does repeat itself, I would have to think that my medical adventures are not over. I do, however, hold out hope that my medical experiences will be deemed complete. I routinely visit my primary-care doctor and both cardiology specialists, and let them monitor my health and the implanted device. They control my pulse rate by remote control, among other things, in order to keep me on borrowed time. The plutonium energy source runs down in about six years of normal use, and the only remedy is a replacement device.

In April 2009, the Veterans Hospital transferred me to the Albany Medical Center for that procedure, and all went well. Although the procedure is considered a minor surgery, I was hospitalized for two days to begin my recovery. Routine follow-up visits every three months will occur at the VA Hospital. They expect no problems for the next six years. Now that is extended borrowed time! The professionals I have encountered along these medical detours of my life have been outstanding in their knowledge and their decorum. How proud they must be at the end of their day for helping all of us.

CHAPTER 4

Taking the Suggested Steps Toward Recovery

I have now been associated with Alcoholics Anonymous for over three decades, and I have to say that had I not been a raging alcoholic, I would have lost the opportunity to live an exciting life. The tenets of the twelve-step program can be adopted by anyone for the betterment of their lives, regardless of their affinity with alcohol or drugs. It has given my life meaning. Most of my understanding of life is due to the experiences I have had in and around Alcoholics Anonymous.

Obviously it would be easier to begin the program, and to understand such a program, if the person was not addicted in his or her thinking when first approaching the program. I say this because people new to this simple program often fear the steps and the perceived process that has proven to be the *only* path to extended and meaningful sobriety and an improved life. All of the detoxification facilities and short-term rehabilitation centers in the world can only point someone in the direction of the AA program. Then growth, change, and progress can begin. If an attempt is made to stay sober after discharge, without AA, it is likely that sobriety will not last. These rehabilitation opportunities can only be expected to safely dry someone out, and introduce him or her to a new way of thinking, simply setting the stage for Alcoholics Anonymous. They are helpful mostly because they physically remove the opportunity for the drinker to drink. Early birds to the program have to find patience while their heads clear and all this new information has a chance to seed itself in one's soggy brain. It's not easy to sit still when the need for a drink is insidiously swirling at the base of the brain while listening to fellow alcoholics who have experienced all of these feelings and much more. It's not easy, but the support of those who have remained sober through this challenging period makes the goal entirely possible.

For instance, the longer the chance is given to the fellowship of Alcoholics Anonymous by attending meetings and not drinking one day at a time, the more likely someone with recovery experience is going to say something that will spark the new person's interest and establish common ground and experience. This is the golden moment, but it can be elusive. Time is needed to assure this moment arises, and the all-important turn of attitude can occur that will open the ears and the mind of the "new guy." This signals the start of meaningful sobriety. The program is simply structured by way of twelve steps suggested to everyone and should be approached one day at a time.

In the **first step**, we admitted we were powerless over alcohol—that our lives had become unmanageable. Personally, this was the hardest step for me, because by admitting I was an alcoholic, I was turning off the flow of booze that was such a large part of my life and routine. It is hard to turn your back on your "best friend," alcohol, when it soothed so many feelings and clouded so many of the realities of life that plagued me. My biggest fear was that the more people that knew I could not drink anymore, meant I would have trouble drinking more!

Admitting my life was unmanageable was a simple process because my life was screwed up beyond belief when I first entered AA on December 8, 1977: Two marriages gone south, DUI's, work problems, money problems, social problems, housing issues, child support complaints, estrangements from other close relatives, nutritional concerns, transportation limitations, health concerns, and long-term security issues. Now when I hear the word "problem" I know, "what causes the problem is the problem." How simple is that? Drinking was the problem, and there I was trying to protect my right to drink at some time in the future, my right to hurt myself with a substance I thought was an asset. In early recovery, it is suggested to stay focused on the real problem and set aside all the issues or troubles that beg to be addressed first. Those solutions fall into place once sobriety takes hold.

The **second step** is that we came to believe that a Power greater than ourselves could restore us to sanity. Believing that a Power greater than myself could restore my sanity was all that was left for me when I finally stopped drinking. I repeatedly failed to correct my patterns of living. To continue to drink was pure insanity in and of itself. I was a failure in every direction of my life, and therefore willing to allow any untried approach to guide me toward success. It is here that many people erroneously think AA religious, when spirituality is really the guiding principle. This is the one step I suggest be tried, or just given a chance until the benefits become tangible. Time and experience in the fellowship will ensure that these benefits are made manifest. Newcomers are encouraged to simply stay sober while working the steps slowly at this early point of an introduction to the program.

The **third step** is to make a decision to turn our will and our lives over to the care of God—as we understand Him. As in the second step, I wasn't doing so great on my own, so why not try it? Many of us have tried to hold on to the idea that we alone are in charge of our lives, but these excuses can delay meaningful improvement as a result of working the program.

Hey, I used to tell people, "I am an occasional drinker—I only drink if I am alone or with someone!"

Excuses of any nature along these lines are no more than convenient rationalizations, and they need to be put in their proper place so that progress can begin. The group process supports the individual, so attending step or discussion meetings is helpful. In the **fourth step**, we make a searching and fearless moral inventory of ourselves. For me, this step required some help in the form of a sponsor, an experienced AA member who I connected with, to help me work through this difficult step. Making an inventory of myself was a daunting thought, because deep down inside I knew what I did, and I hesitated to share those details with anyone. I feared being judged and dismissed as wholly unworthy of my sponsor's support. This step is critical; however, as it helps clear the wreckage of the past and establish a starting point for living a sober life. The concept of sponsorship proves effective when put into practice. It creates a much-needed measure of privacy between the two people. It also allows for the exchange of experiences that prove similar in framework and outcome, even while circumstantially different.

Sincerely, when speaking at meetings, long-term recovering members often speak frankly about their drunken pasts and the humiliating consequences, thus helping the "new guys" identify with similar experiences, lessening apprehensions about this process. Attending meetings often helps bring this concept together, because the more stories shared and heard, the more the group, and each individual, benefits from the process of identification. Many of these stories also bring a large measure of humor to the group, which is refreshing and calming.

I do not mean to infer that working the steps is a quick and easy process.

Months and years are often devoted to meetings and social gatherings at AA clubs or coffee shops so that interaction with recovering members will allow for some personal understanding of the steps, in addition to the gradual clearing of the mind. Slowly, everything begins to make sense. Long-term abuse of alcohol results in muddled thinking; lucidity does not return quickly. It only takes a few hours to get seriously drunk if you are trying, but physically and mentally it can take months for the damage to brain and body to be repaired. Time, an unpopular word in the program, is important for a good chance at meaningful recovery.

The **fifth step** is that we admit to God, to ourselves, and to another human being the exact nature of our wrongs. I practiced this step while working on my fourth, which appeared to be a natural process for me. I had an intimate understanding of God personally, so I was not delayed in trying to search out the meaning of God or a Higher Power. Many members struggle with admitting to God the exact nature of their wrongs. The Higher Power concept is usually easy to explain, but sometimes impossible to translate. The gradual evolution of the individual's spiritual understanding, and the ensuing willingness to trust its benevolence, again, blooms with time.

The **sixth step** is that we were entirely ready to have God remove all these defects of character, and the **seventh step** is to humbly ask Him to remove our shortcomings. For me, these steps meant to open up, relax, and try to believe that things would get better if I could act on the suggestion to "let go and let God," a phrase I've now heard thousands of times all around the fellowship. In my own recovery continuum, I was about a year sober when seriously working on these middle steps. Timing is different from person to person, and therefore not predictable. There is literature available to explain each of the steps that are available in the rooms of Alcoholics Anonymous, and everyone serious about finding sobriety and a better life can study it.

The **eighth step** is to make a list of all persons we have harmed, and become willing to make amends to them all, and the **ninth step** is to make direct amends to such people wherever possible, except when to do so would injure them or others. Memories come and go in the early stages of recovery. It is important to go slowly when listing the people harmed, as omissions are sometimes made in haste. Calm thinking and not projecting negative reactions to future direct amends is essential. When the list is complete, time can be taken to prepare to make amends, "except when to do so would injure them or others." "Become willing" means what it says. A sponsor can help in making a long-term plan to address each amends in an orderly fashion. These are steps, not leaps.

In terms of taking action to make the actual amends, the words "wherever possible" allow us to approach this step with caution and thoughtfulness. Do not crash forward, creating the possibility of injury to yourself or others. For instance, children's ages and maturity should be considered carefully. It is often best to wait until they grow up and adjust beyond your harm before you dump on them in an attempt to advance yourself in the program. Children are usually pleased with the way things are going in sobriety and will tend not to reflect on the past if it is not suggested. Common sense and talking these matters over with other AA members is a good way to moderate these issues. Other parents or relatives need to be consulted as well.

The **tenth step** is to continue to take personal inventory, and when we are wrong, promptly admit it. The tenth step is perfectly good and sound advice to anyone anywhere. My experience with this had been a guiding light in my life for over thirty years. Even though I hate confrontation, I have learned to act immediately when I realize that I have wronged someone, or even misspoke.

Procrastination amplifies the problem. Get things straightened out as soon as humanly possible, and your peace of mind has a far greater chance to survive a correctable problem or issue that would just fester if left alone. I think this step is intended to help you keep an even keel in your emotions and in your future. It is very practical advice for anyone.

The **eleventh step** is to seek through prayer and meditation to improve our conscious contact with God as we understand Him, praying only for the knowledge of His will for us and the power to carry that out. This step is so near the end that I suspect most of us have needed time to get here, so we have had the chance to sober up physically, begin thinking clearly, and experience changes that have crept into our lives. This is the comforting part of the entire program, and it will help you feel what is now going on. Without too much guidance on your part, improvements are realized and blessings can be recognized now that you have devoted all this time to your initial recovery. There is no qualifier here; we all grow and have changed! It should make you emotional during prayer and medication if you honestly look at your early gifts from the program and the fellowship.

The final step, the **twelfth step**, is having had a spiritual awakening as the result of these steps, we tried to carry this message to alcoholics, and practice these principles in all our affairs. In order to keep sobriety, you must give it away to others. There are many ways in life to feel good about this suggestion and to "practice these principles" in your day-to-day lives. Family, friends and co-workers can rely on your advice and judgment when alcohol problems close in on them and those who are near to them. They can also rely on you. This is your chance to help someone to find the things and the feelings you are now experiencing in life, supported by the program. It is literally a chance to be a hero. No matter what you choose to invest here, I guarantee you that your life will be so improved, you will think that you have started a whole new life over again. An out of control life is now stable and productive. Troubles and issues may still come, but you are far better equipped to handle them while maintaining your sobriety. The major problem is under control: drinking. You can once again dare to dream of good things to happen to you in your life.

Life after being introduced to Alcoholics Anonymous is forever altered. First of all, AA will ruin your drinking, and probably the drinking of those closest to you.

It is unconscionable to just sit there and drink, although certainly not impossible, after you have been schooled in the rooms of AA. You have to feel a little guilty about having admitted you are an alcoholic and then picking up a drink again, disregarding everything you learned that is good about the program and applicable to you. When I did this, I found myself hiding where no one knew me, usually in the lowest of bars, in order to be able to compare myself with others who were "worse than me." This is somehow seen as justification for a drunk to be drinking. As long as you can point to someone else, you can justify your own drinking for a time, subject to the progression of alcoholism that will alter your "position" in the bar as time goes by. That is when reality begins to get a foothold as you slither down the chart of alcoholic progression.

I actually succeeded in not drinking for over four years after my first start in AA, which was also beyond the treatment programs I had experienced at the Albany, New York, VA Hospital. After a year in the program, while working in a halfway house, I married my third wife Stacey, who was also recovering. I later found a great job selling insurance for a fraternal insurance company. This job called for me to travel occasionally, and a few years later I would try drinking while out of town because "no one knew me," and I thought I could get away with it.

Our marriage was created in sobriety, and wisely my third wife Stacey chose sobriety, rather than being challenged by a relationship with someone who had returned to drinking alcohol. She dutifully arranged for an intervention by other sober members of AA to help me, as I mentioned before, but I resisted, only to find myself moving out at Stacey's insistence. I found an apartment alone, and my drinking increased while my job performance and reliability suffered. I began associating with other former AA members that were also drinking, and together we were headed in the wrong direction. These associations rarely last for long because of the negative forces at work at the same time.

When I finally lost my job selling insurance products, I ended up working in the woods again in order to survive. Generally, things declined and relationships were problematic, as I found myself living out of a rented trailer. I realized that life was empty and I couldn't see a reasonable relationship in life ahead again. I really was a slow learner, but I was able to clean up my act and try to get back into going to meetings and not drink, *one day at a time.*

I felt that I was at a turning point in my life because I was approaching forty years old and I wasn't settled into anything that would someday allow me to retire. Since I needed a car and a good job, I decided to apply for work as a car salesman, as salesmen were known to get demonstrator cars as a benefit of selling them.

This plan surprisingly worked, and I was hired by a local Chevrolet dealer in 1983 and went to meetings, trying to begin to get my life back on track.

Early success again bred contempt, and I was gradually back to "limited" drinking with my fellow salesmen and friends within a year and a half. I quit my first store to go to another dealership some thirty miles away in order to get another fresh start, somehow thinking that a geographical change would fix my life. Problem was, I was bringing myself to the new location, and this became my new pattern of trying to manage my life while still drinking. I began to bounce around, selling cars all over the place for several years before I finally surrendered again. This was after becoming involved with my fourth wife Betty and finding a good reason to straighten up, in addition to the obvious.

We were married on September 5, 1993, and with her love and support, along with AA, I am still going strong. My job stabilized as a result of my sobriety, so Betty and I together began to plan and build a new home in the country on more than four acres that I had found near my work site. With my experience in the woods, I was able to clear our land and get it ready for construction with little assistance.

This project was all consuming, as I ended up supervising the overall building of the house and final development of the land, while selling cars on a full schedule. Money was flying around in every direction, and we finally completed the project a year later and $20,000 over budget. Last minute creative financing was arranged in order to close on the final deal, and we moved into our new place at the end of 1994. What a great feeling to live in a home I had designed and invested so much of myself into! It gave me great pride to just take it all in from time to time, even though our finances were stretched thin as an end result of the overall project costs. Watching herds of deer walk across our land day and night pushed aside any pressing financial concerns. I felt that things could only get better.

I was always willing to work harder and longer in order to keep our heads above water, until my first heart attack and the impending decline in my overall health and physical capabilities that began to impact our lives. The five-month break from earning money after my cancer operation and chemotherapy would prove critical in our overall finances, and the struggles began just to hold on to the house. By 2003, I could no longer keep up with all the payments and expenses and we had to sell the house and property. I rewarded us by getting the best apartment around, but it was never the same. This was truly an opportunity lost, as I had also planned to use the equity in the property to augment my retirement income some day.

By the time we had to sell the house, my physical disabilities were also limiting me from all the usual upkeep chores. I settled down about moving into an apartment because others would now handle the maintenance. My job had been going well, and I had taken on additional duties helping to manage one of the sales departments along with selling duties at the same time. These circumstances made me feel good about myself, until a new general manager took over the three-store operation and decided he did not want me. I had worked there for seven and a half years straight and was canned without notice or stated reason. You've got to love the car business! I took two months off to personally process these events and my feelings, and then started working for another Chevrolet store for the two and a half years preceding my total disability and retirement, on December 12, 2006. This period of time proved rewarding to me because of the people there and the experiences I had the chance to live with them. This experience taught me when one door closes, another one will open if you trust in Him.

I have seen this principle at work in AA always. Through all of my life upsets and adjustments during this period, my sobriety never wavered. I am solid in my life and have processed all of these circumstances without the slightest inclination to return to drinking. I have been thinking clearly and soberly now for over sixteen years and enjoy the knowledge I have gathered over my thirty-plus years in Alcoholics Anonymous. I believe that learning about AA can change lives. That is an overall thirty-year observation that holds true in my own life and many others throughout the organization. The difference in the quality of life enhanced by AA approaches the indescribable because of the multiple and far-reaching effects the program has imparted on others and me.

To avoid this program and fellowship, for whatever insane reason a drunk can conjure up, would be a tragedy of historic proportions. This can be the turning point that will define life, or a miserable death for someone who is living with an alcohol problem they think is incurable. I joke about my health history and my terminal outlook "on borrowed time," but when I do go, it will be sober and it will be worthwhile because of the way AA has taught me to think and to live. I have no regrets because I have done everything possible "to make amends except when to do so would injure them or others." When you have peace of mind, your daily challenges are manageable, and your future is bright and open to blessings you haven't prayed for. My life today is filled with love and understanding, both giving and receiving. I look forward to each and every day. The sky is the limit, and the sky is filled with Angels that help me with any challenge I face today.

There is plenty of room in this fellowship once you decide that you have the desire to stop drinking. With that as a starting point, you can begin to live a good life and find the ways you need to correct the past. You have hundreds of friends you haven't met yet that are all willing to help you. You just have to take the first step . . . the rest we will help you with!

CHAPTER 5

Meaningful Relationships Are at the Core of My Success

As I near the end of my life, I realize I have a long and diverse history to look back upon when I ponder what life has been all about for me. The meaning of life has been the relationships I have formed or enhanced since I got sober. Before my sobriety, friendships and acquaintances, for the most part, were shallow at best.

My relatives had a strained relationship with me because I was not reliable, truthful, or available for them when it was important. It is difficult, even today, when I remember the disappointment I saw so many times on the faces of the people close to me who didn't deserve to be treated that way. I think it is important to share some of the great relationships I have experienced in order to demonstrate the really important results of using the AA program in one's life and what it means near the end. First of all, when I finally got sober, my sister Judy and I were able to reunite and reform the closest of relations. My drinking had kept me away from her life for a few years because, by my own rules, I would not show up drinking or with my world in a mess. Her sincere interest in my life and well-being were displayed to me every time I saw her or spoke to her from my home. She would always listen to me intently and respond articulately to anything that was going on in my life.

Judy was always the first one I would call when something good happened to me because it gave her so much joy. She was also the first to strongly suggest I retire because of my declining health, and as it turned out, I did retire just four days before I lost her. My strongest memory of her now is when she told me in the intensive care unit she was scared because she knew her health had plummeted and she faced death within days. Her ability to talk had been greatly limited due to a stroke, but she was clear when she spoke to me about this.

I reassured her she had great doctors and nurses taking care of her, as a way to try to comfort her, while I combed her hair with my fingers and tried to soothe her.

Her vital organs would soon fail, and she died in her sleep on the morning of December 16, 2006. Fourteen years of deep love and companionship with her in my sobriety and a lifetime of fond memories are truly a highlight of my entire life. Further enhancing this relationship, her husband of forty-three years, Mike Joyce, has been like a brother to me. We will always share great memories together because of Judy and the special relationship we all shared. Their son Mark and his wife Megan, along with their newborn son Evan Allen Joyce, are all so special to me that the words escape me to describe how important they all are.

Soon after I was reunited with my sister in Massachusetts, I was able to get together with my oldest daughter Kimberly Jean, who never understood why I stayed away for so long. To her, my drinking would not have mattered if she could only spend time with me. I had missed out on many years of her life, including school, college, jobs, and her marriage because I was embarrassed about whom I was while drinking and the condition of my life. We were quickly drawn together by our unspoken bond and began seeing each other again. Also, for the last ten years I have been able to share my family and myself with her beautiful daughter Alyssa Paige, who lights up my life as my only granddaughter. She had been born the day before my cancer operation to remove my right lung, and because of that we came close to never meeting at all, so I am especially grateful for her today.

Kimberly Jean also brokered a deal to help me get back in touch with her younger sister Heather Lynn, who justifiably was not all that excited to see me again. Divorcing her mother and being separated from her when she was just a child had built some pretty ugly walls between us. My visitation and support of her had been sporadic, and her memories were all negative. She has since allowed some visits and a good deal of correspondence, and we have been able to grow together on a limited basis. She now lives and works successfully in Colorado, and I continue to try to enhance our relationship as time allows. I am proud of her for opening those doors.

My relationships with my three stepsons, now in their mid-forties, were stabilized due to my sobriety. They are always showing me their love, and they are all special to me because they honor their mother and respect me now. My only grandson Justin, who is now twenty, asked me when he was eleven years old to promise not to use cigarettes after my cancer operation, and I wrote a note for him to hold saying that I would not smoke again. This would end my struggles with smoking, but I can take little credit, as is deserving of those who quit on their own. Although I was physically addicted, I was also physically incapable of smoking because of my health, and my non-smoking time easily continues.

God really has a sense of humor because He made sure I could not smoke again as a result of the damage to my throat that continues even today. Justin's concern for me and the bravery he displayed in asking me to stop is what I will always remember and take with me. All four boys have always extended their hand and hugged me at every meeting, no matter where we are. Once you have something like this, how can you live without it? These are the real things that make me not drink and go to meetings, my fuel for sobriety.

I was able to reunite with a friend I had met in 1983, when I first started working in auto sales, whose name was Billy Osher. Billy was four years younger than I, but we both served in Vietnam (he as a medic), and we respected our selling profession and agreed most of the time on process and procedure about our work. I was able to work closely with him for five years, including the time during my heart attacks and cancer ordeal. He had in fact spent seven hours at the hospital when I was being operated on, to support my family members and demonstrate his concern for me. He enjoyed visiting my wife and me in our home in the country. Billy was an active sportsman who played baseball, football, basketball, golf, jogging, and was in great physical health by all outward signs. He was friendly, caring, and well respected by family, customers, co-workers, and many friends all around town. In one of his last meetings with our management, he had voiced his concern about my health problems and had admitted that it was affecting him greatly. The events of September 11, 2001, concerned and angered him because we worked closely with a gentleman from Pakistan whom he felt protective of, given the circumstances of the hour.

On April 12, 2002, Billy died of an unexpected heart attack at the age of fifty-four after his morning jog. An autopsy would reveal that he had been experiencing silent heart attacks for some time, and nothing could have been done to save him at the end. The depth of his kindness and caring were constant feelings that I was privileged to enjoy while being associated with him for over ten years of my sobriety. I continued to surround myself with his words and pictures that I treasure in fond remembrance of a great friend in every sense. His tragic and early death reminds me to live each day that I am granted and to enjoy the fullness of all of my relationships.

There were several other guys and gals from that first automobile experience that I also continue to talk to and occasionally visit that bring peace and good feelings to me. Most of my relationships prior to this time had been without much meaning, and these people helped me to celebrate sobriety in the real world by liking me. We easily joke about my escapades and our memories of my drinking days from up to twenty-five years ago. It is relationships like these that help keep me sober, while I remember my past without judgments or faults being pointed out.

They seem to accept me today, and I value their close friendships.

Another friend of over twenty years, Edwin Vosburgh, had always stayed in touch and had actually worked with me in three different stores over the years. We played golf hundreds of times and enjoyed each other's company along with our golfing buddy, Bob Kelley. Ed was my best man when I married Betty (my fourth and current wife), and I truly valued his friendship. He was able to retire a year before me because he was a year older, as I always reminded him, and we had talked on the phone frequently. I did not see him often after his retirement because my golfing days were done due to my physical limitations, but our friendship never ended. In August 2008, Eddie died from prostate cancer just a few days after my last visit with him. He had fought the ultimate cancer fight but tired at the end, finally letting go with dignity.

I had always felt close enough with Ed to talk about anything that was on my mind, and he was always helpful and did not judge me. The value of a true friend like this is not easily described because our relationship brought me comfort and understanding without any limitations. I respected Ed for his maturity and life accomplishments, and I feel that my life would not have been as full as it is now without his friendship and all the memories and good times we had shared. Ed Vosburgh was a true gift in my life, never to be forgotten.

During the last ten years of working in the car business, I was able to meet hundreds of good people from all walks of life, and I found so many of them interesting and meaningful in my day-to-day affairs. I was able to observe their respect for my age and experience, and I was proud to be responsible for them in work and in our friendships. In the last two years, I also saw the pain on their faces as my health declined, and I knew their concerns were sincere. Many times, my days were filled with my co-workers offering to do some of my work so that I would not overdo it. The depth of their humanity, kindness, and humility has been remarkable. I now look forward to having my cars serviced so that I can roam around and visit with everyone who is still working there.

During my twenty-four years in the auto business, I have met owners, officers of the companies, department managers, accountants, office personnel, service managers and technicians, financial managers, salesmen and women, sales managers, clerical staff, and maintenance people who have all added to my life.

Working with them and their diverse backgrounds and personalities have given me a fullness of life. The diversity of the thousands of customers I dealt with every day over all those years also enriched my life experience. Many of them would become close personal friends that I still stay in touch with today. Some of them were a part of my real life to begin with.

The most important relationship of all is with my wife, Betty Boop, who has stood the test of time through the many ups and downs in my life including my conduct in sobriety and before. She has never given up on me and has literally been by my side through all my adventures and illnesses over the last twenty-one years. Betty has always taken the time to listen to me and to try to understand my feelings and actions that sometimes fly in the face of normalcy. I tend to be outspoken to a fault (I think because of my sister Judy), and she occasionally helps me backtrack in order to modify my words and actions in order to make things right. Our time together has proven to be the best years of my life because of her love and understanding. There could never be another wife for me because there will never be another Betty Boop! (I only call her my "current wife" to keep her on her toes.) I can now only pray that my life will contribute to her security forever, as she deserves only the best in our final days.

I couldn't write about Betty without pointing out how involved and important she is in the lives of our five adult children and two grandchildren. Betty is in constant touch with all of them on a daily basis and provides moral support and wisdom to add to their lives. All of their families and friendships are enhanced with the experience and love she contributes. She has always carried on the traditions of her parents in a somewhat old-fashioned way, a way that should be better known. Unconditional love has been hers all of her life, and that is what she always communicates to our entire family. She is a blessing for us all.

The point of discussing these personal relationships is that they remind me, in a way, of the total lack of meaningful relationships I had before sobriety caught up to me. I want others to know that all this and more is possible—after you get a grip on the program of Alcoholics Anonymous and begin to make changes in your life as recommended by the twelve steps of the program. When I look at my life and ponder the approaching end of it, I have to tell you that the most important thing in my world is the love, understanding, and mutual respect I now experience with almost everyone in my current life. You have to ask yourself what you are going to take with you when you die, and you should listen carefully to the answer you hear.

It certainly isn't possessions, property, or things! How you feel about others and how they feel about you is spiritual, and *that* is what you will be taking with you.

There are a lot of other interesting things I could be doing with my retirement other than writing a book, but I think that many people really need to know some of this stuff! Life isn't going to slow down and wait for you to catch up.

That said, spirituality should be our focus now, as it trumps everything else in life and promotes meaning and rewards along the path of life. When are you going to start? Since I have embraced these ideals, I breathe easier, sleep better, and enjoy my life because of its fullness. I have been able to write many letters, tributes, and poems to friends and relatives that express my honest feelings about them. I recently wrote a letter to an AA friend, and I told her simply how beautiful she is when she enters the room and how important she is to our group. She has since written to me about how I am a "treasured friend." It is beautiful to know that you can love someone for the right reasons and feel that sentiment in return. I personally cannot think of a better way to walk through life. What on earth could make you feel better than that?

Each relationship I have also supports my sobriety. The more I develop good relationships, the more protection I afford myself from wandering afield. I feel I cannot disappoint everyone in my life by doing something stupid, so I give myself more time to grow and more time to experience life on borrowed time, staying sober another day. Alcoholics Anonymous addresses spirituality in great depth, but I wanted you to know how profoundly it has changed my life from a point near suicide to a way of life where I can celebrate my life and loves.

Oh yes, suicide is very real among those of us with a drinking problem because alcohol is a depressive drug, often taken to great excess. Many times the distinction of suicide vs. accidental overdose is blurred and of no importance after death anyway. How many times did you approach these thoughts? "Never again" can be your answer today, if you only give AA a try.

When it is time to die, I am sure I, too, will be scared as hell, but I will also be ready to join those who have gone before me. I like to tell people to be sure to tell someone how you really feel about them, and you will be armed to live another day with gratitude for a sober way of living.

I am going out on a limb here, but I want to observe that there are lots of people that do not drink problematically who could use this simple program to improve their lives and the depth of the meaning in life that can be experienced through serious relationships built on common respect. This twelve-step program can be adapted for those who have eating disorders, weight control problems, co-dependency issues, any other obsessive-compulsive disorder, or the early indications of problems.

If you recognize someone you love heading down a slippery slope, should you try to intervene, or wait for the crash at the bottom of the hill? Life is too short, and it deserves your participation by helping yourself or someone you care about in a mission designed to improve life itself. Inaction or lack of responsibility will certainly prolong the pain, so I pray that you will get into action where and when it is appropriate. Remember too, that fellowship is needed to bring all things together. AA does that the best!

When groups of people with a common bond get together and share their ideas, problems, and thoughts, magic just happens! If you don't know that, I can't explain it to you. It just happens! When I was drinking, I didn't want anyone to know what was going on in my life or how I felt, nor would I have listened to anyone if they had my solution in hand. I was hell-bent to solve all my problems alone. Fat chance. My problems kept getting bigger and more complex by the day.

"If you want what we have and are willing to go to any length to get it . . . then there are certain steps you must take." You will never get out of the fog, until you let go absolutely. So it is up to you, I can't do anymore . . .

Chapter 6

Perhaps the Hopes and Prayers Along the Way, the Ambitions and the Dreams

It has often been said one's life passes before them at or near the point of death, according to many who have been resuscitated or in some way been brought back to life medically. This thought brings me to my wish that, given a little notice, I would like the opportunity to appear in a huge theater-in-the-round just before I die, so I could see and possibly address all of the people I have encountered in my lifetime. Sadly, a great part of the audience for me would be the spirits of those passed, as that segment of my life grows larger every year that I remain on borrowed time. How strange it is to consider that I was supposed to die nearly ten years ago and then to think of all those close to me I have lost during that period.

If the theater could be arranged, I would be able to see all of my relatives for generations before me that made an influence in my genes and my background.

Think of the kids I grew up with in elementary, junior, and high schools, trade schools, and community college. The rush of memories about my parents and sister on the hilltop, all the years of adolescence and beyond. Add the hundreds of men I went through boot camp with and served with in France and Germany for two years. I would want all those whom I served with that lost their lives in Vietnam, so they would hear of my admiration for all of them and my envy of their heroism.

I would also want the people I worked with in many walks of my life while working in the woods, stock brokering, insurance sales, odds and ends, and finally, those from my twenty-four years in car sales. All of my co-workers, supervisors, and customers by the thousand could be present to see me one last time. Then, of course, there would be that section of my wives (four) and girlfriends (?). There would have to be a special section for my closest relatives and friends who have died, as they meant so much to me. My warmest memories are for those I can only whisper to now, and I would want them all to meet each other to form a common bond around me . . . like the wings of an Angel and the arms of my Higher Power protecting me.

Where would I begin? With the fun memories, the learning, and growing pains, the "first" experiences, or the early sadnesses and disappointments? Perhaps the hopes and prayers along the way, the ambitions and the dreams. How they have changed without warning over all my years. Not all the times were good, nor were all the experiences. I must remember the shameful moments and acts. Those times I still cannot explain, and sometimes cannot remember, due to the effects my drinking had on my brain. Many lives were affected and need my apologies, not my excuses. I remember many broken promises and damaged hearts. I would need to confess my wrongs while asking for those to understand the changing times of my life that influenced many of my decisions and actions that resulted in bad feelings, injury, and disrupted lives. My mental problems and alcohol abuse clouded my thinking and caused me to make so many errors in judgment.

My two young daughters, Kimberly Jean and Heather Lynn, were probably the greatest victims of my addictions because I needed to drink more than I could make myself do the right things for my first family, which only lasted for seven years before divorce. I was forced to move beyond my family responsibilities by the power of addiction and post-traumatic stress disorder that gripped my life for many years. This propelled me into a search for new surroundings and new people, away from Massachusetts and the problems I had created. I always needed "family" and would spend seventeen years trying to fit in somewhere in New York where I could feel comfortable. That search would create two more failed marriages with stepchildren involved. Meanwhile, the girls were growing up and going to schools without their father's input in any way. Their mother and grandparents would have to provide all their guidance, love, and sense of family.

Many years would pass before we could love again. Perhaps the theater could provide some explanations, some understanding. This really hurts me deeply, even today.

What I would want most in this theater is to be able to try to relate what was going on from my personal perspective, in hopes of finding a measure of personal understanding and maybe even forgiveness in part. Although my feelings were shrouded in alcohol, it did not mean that I did not feel. The depressions for many years were deep, nearly suicidal at times, because there was so much behind me and so little I could envision in front of me. It is difficult to propel yourself forward when there is such a large anchor tied to your behind. The tenets of the AA program and the fellowship it inspires would assist in these areas once I finally found meaningful sobriety, but as time goes by, the bad memories are frequently rekindled and cause concerns anew. Not every wrong in life has an amends, of this I am sure. Therefore, the complete wreckage, for me, cannot always be cleared. I must remain ready to do what I can if the circumstances change.

Somehow I believe that by addressing all of the thousands of people in my life "in the round," I would find understanding by bringing them all together in the overall story of Bob Allen. Maybe the people with good memories could help me win over those with not-so-good memories, or perhaps the reverse would bring the good ones down! Most of all, those who have passed, and now probably know it all, would be the best people to tie it all together and help me win over the audience. That might sound like a pipe dream, but it would certainly tidy up the wake of destruction I created. During the last two decades, I have succeeded in most areas of my life and now feel comfortable that I at least try to the best of my ability to do the right things, say the right things, and lead by example for a change.

The reason I would want this all to happen in the round is so I could keep talking and turning the stage until I was able to win them all over. This is something only a salesman would think of . . .

One of the hardest things to explain about life is the twists and turns that guide your actions, decisions, and the ultimate direction of your life. I have looked at things clearly, when sober, and have been convinced my decisions were correct and based on accurate input, only to find out, for reasons unknown to me, I was totally wrong. Time and again, "letting go and letting God" would have been the right way to approach the decision. Then things work out for the better, but it is so difficult to let go of the reigns. Finding a faith or Higher Power you can rely on allows you to fall on gentle hands, making decisions not as important as you may have thought. The ability to discern the proper timing of a decision also falls squarely within these parameters. Let go, and the correct timing will develop on its own. When you do fall onto gentle hands, it is the greatest feeling and comfort you can experience. Practicing this method is what is difficult. When you try not to get excited and rush things, it becomes second nature to let life flow, and you will then look back and see the timing is often *perfected by your patience!*

Try to look back in your history and remember a decision you *didn't* make where everything worked out fine, and you may discover your own experience needed to endorse and retry this ideal. It works! Remember, all good things require some action, so tender that thought as you go forward. I have always been one to do my "homework" before a decision, meeting, or application, and that process has made smooth many stressful times of my life in recent decades. When you research a new event, you will be armed with knowledge that will guide you through any process and help make your nerves calm under the normal stress we all feel, especially when addressing something new in your life. Think of the basic tenets of education, and you will see it teaches you how to research and prepare for life, not just to provide all the answers that you must commit to memory. Doing your *homework* will guide you through the unknowns as life unfolds. When you know the answers because of your research, it becomes easier to ask the right questions when trying to guide others to support your personal goals. Any experienced salesman will quickly endorse this ideal because life experiences support every word of it. When you are not ready to negotiate, you will lose. Selling automobile products has introduced me to many different types of people in the public at large. In the selection, demonstration, negotiation, and delivery process of selling cars and trucks, the raw truth of each personality seems to find its way to the surface. What you can learn from them all is astounding, as long as you are paying attention. The accumulation of this information makes different all of those who have devoted their time and efforts to this profession.

Once you become a part of that kind of a selling team for some years, you get hooked on continued association with those who have experienced the truths that emerge from these activities. Bottom line (that's car talk), you learn volumes about a person engaged in large dollar negotiations, and it is not all good.

Much of the general public tends to look down on car salespersons; probably because the buyers know that the tricks they like to employ don't work against a savvy salesperson. It is often thought salespeople are dishonest, when in reality, we spend much of our time and expertise defending our companies from dirty tricks.

Good, solid companies earn a decent profit, and thereafter are positioned to provide reliable after-sale service, while supporting all of those who make up their teams and pay their share to the community they serve.

Why then should they be expected to sell cars at a loss? I guess, at the end of the day, it's a love-hate relationship between sales representatives and some customers. Let me assure you: The customer who wins is the customer who treats the salesperson with a moderate level of respect and acknowledges some profit has to exist in order to solidify a transaction and support future reliable service for the products sold. Just trying to be a pain in the ass should not qualify someone for additional discounts beyond those afforded nice customers.

If you are shopping for a vehicle and you feel the comments above do not apply to your adventure, then I would suggest you may have selected the wrong place to shop. If someone is trying to take advantage of you, move on. There are countless good companies and good salespeople waiting to serve you where these principles apply. Your satisfaction should be assumed. Your treatment, respectful.

When looking back through my life, I recall most of the time I wrongly valued myself by the results and accomplishments of the job I had at the time, and of course, how much money I had earned. There was a time when I did not consider the relationships I participated in and all the good that flowed from them. So you can see that a swing in the economy, the weather, or some other stress I had no control over would alter the way I felt about myself, and therefore treated myself.

During my car-selling years, I had transitioned into sobriety, and as a result, my mood swings and upsets moderated as I began to accept myself and others concerning the events of life that churned around me.

It is hard to look back without remembering some of the tricks I employed in order to survive in work and at home. It was completely normal through several periods of time for me to go to and return to work pretty well smashed. Then, out of routine, I would sell a car that was going to be picked up the following day by someone I would not recognize by then! The trick involved here was simply to say I needed another copy of their license and I would then go the office to research the delivery, review my negotiations, and proceed to affect the delivery, as my mind would slowly pick up the pieces from the previous day. These types of events were a product of blackouts, caused by bathing my brain in alcohol for so long, and so frequently. I would be able to perform normal duties out of routine, while not being conscious enough to exactly remember much.

Speaking of blackouts, try to imagine what many addicted, active alcoholics have participated in without a clear memory of what they were doing. Some of the most successful recovery stories from members in Alcoholics Anonymous include astounding recalls that prompted them to try recover over mystery.

A locally famous speaker at AA meetings can be quoted as saying, "I knew it was time for help when I found myself waking up with people I would normally not have wanted to speak to."

You never know! That turned out to be the catalyst that drove her to AA and motivated her to devour most of the writings associated with that recovery program and led her into sponsoring many new women in the program. She would die sober twenty-seven years later while working at a recovery center as a counselor-supervisor and also working privately in the same profession. She was one of the few people I know who *got the program* on the first try after many years of active, problematic drinking. This, I think, leaves open the door to anyone who is really ready and willing to go to any lengths to get sober. There are no limits to the number of tries you can take, but I thought it would be nice for you to know the first time can really work—if you become dedicated to it, work the program as it was designed, and will be recommended by current members. I am not a good example of that kind of success. Hopefully, my failures at grasping the program early on will be examples of what not to do.

I should also mention that, as much as I personally believe that Alcoholics Anonymous is the only answer, there are a few— very few— persons who find enough faith or muster the self discipline to walk away from their alcoholism. I say this reluctantly because the odds are greatly against you, and the penalties can be fatal for you, or worse yet, fatal for some other innocent person or persons whose lives cross your path while you were looking for direction through the bottom of a bottle.

You should have enough experience trying to stop on your own before now to understand my concerns. There are thousands of people who have tried this and ended up in AA with more baggage than they can handle. There are just as many who will never make it back to AA. At the end of the day, the AA fellowship is for people who want it, not need it. *Please* decide carefully. Alcoholics Anonymous will help you find a better way of life, while alternative solutions will only dry you out—if they work at all. If you buy a book that promises a cure, you are really lost and out twenty bucks!

The first step to a successful recovery is to admit you are an alcoholic, and that is a life-altering statement. Internally, you are forced to turn off the source of your pain relief, your inhibition remover, and your greatest hobby. It's damn difficult to cross that bridge, but there are no shortcuts! This step is critical to get away from the input of alcohol, in order to allow the beginning of the mental adjustments and learning needed to proceed in building one's sobriety. The greatest number of "slips" heard of in the fellowship usually occurs in the early period because you have to truly get a handle on who you are and what drinking has been doing to you before progress can be expected. If you still think your life is manageable, then the program has nowhere to take root. The program suggests a series of building blocks to use. Time is needed to digest these concepts, while learning new life habits and schedules. It is all possible, and there is nothing to lose in helping someone find the first open door by calling for help in your community and encouraging them to follow through. It all begins in the rooms for me.

Personally, without getting a start in this direction, my life and existence would have deteriorated beyond repair. Being head strong, I had entrenched myself in habitual behavior that was increasingly pulling me down to levels I knew nothing about. My decent upbringing, good solid education, and great parental influence were being eroded by the effects of alcohol because I was *addicted*. Even the many good life experiences I had had were not influential enough for me to curb an appetite for drinking that was producing serious negative results, time after time. I can't explain this except to say alcoholism can easily take over a life and take you out of the driver's seat altogether. I shudder when I think of all the people doing hard time for crimes they don't even remember committing and can't begin to justify their actions based on their personal memories because of their addiction and their unwillingness to get help before these things can happen. Today I can allow God to drive me where I need to be.

Unspeakable crimes have been committed by some of the nicest people around because they didn't find the solutions available from Alcoholics Anonymous and the simple twelve-step program of suggestions. This fellowship of recovering alcoholics will coach, encourage, and help anyone along who desires to stop drinking and is willing to help him or herself. There may be another way, but I have chosen to live freely and to try to improve my family and myself on this voyage. I have taken the risks, and I have paid the price. I choose today to stay in recovery with AA. It is the best decision made in a lifetime of turbulence.

Currently, my life is filled with experience and understanding, instead of confinement and degradation. I don't have to look far to know why. I was lucky enough to be introduced to AA, and I accidentally got a hold of the program in due time. This is what has changed the lives of millions of people headed in the wrong direction, and I was lucky enough to find a little room for myself in the local program. You don't have to make up stories about drinking; just look around or read a newspaper. Think of the damages caused by alcohol through the people under the influence day after day. Try to justify that after you learn that about ten percent of people drink problematically in the first place. Ninety percent of the population doesn't contribute to the damages! I found that if you drink, you think everybody drinks being that you don't go to places that don't serve alcohol because "you don't like those places." When you drink, you look for ways to justify your drinking, and you don't focus on the negative results and the negative effect it has on our society. You certainly don't want to be told that ninety percent of the world's population does not drink like you. We were not really meant to live our lives this way, but some of us just need a little help to get going in the right direction—away from the train wreck.

After forty-six years of hard work that I enjoyed, I have been forced to retire because of my overall health concerns and disabling work abilities. Things are different now, but I was able to easily adapt to my new life. This was due in great part to my understanding of life after sixty-six rather unusual years. My health is stable, considering all things, my family supportive, and my many friends from work and AA are still good friends in the truest sense. I will always joke about being on borrowed time, because that concept has kept it real for me and has made the ups and downs along the way manageable, even humorous at times.

Modern medical technology and those dedicated to researching and applying new ideas have changed my world and the health outlooks of scores of others with cancer and heart problems. I can appreciate being alive today because of all I have gone through, and am therefore better off than most who are unaware. Sobriety is at the forefront of my success. Alcoholics Anonymous makes that all possible. You don't have to take my word for it— the doors are open and all are welcome.

CHAPTER 7

Let Me Try to Answer That for You . . .

I am not the final expert on alcoholism, except perhaps for the drinking part, but I have learned a lot since my first AA meeting over thirty-two years ago.

Because I do not hide my personal alcoholic history, I am asked questions frequently. Therefore, I would like to advance my answers to some popular questions, according to my own experience and recovery process. I hope this will help someone to understand the mysteries of alcoholism and Alcoholics Anonymous, and get them started in the right direction of recovery, if and when they qualify for membership (the only requirement for membership is the desire to stop drinking).

1. "If I only have two drinks a day, do you think I should be concerned?"

If you ask me that question, then you are already concerned. It would be important for you to review why you set limits to begin with. If there is nothing significant and you can maintain absolute control of your life and don't experience bad things, then it is probably okay, at least for today. My greatest concern about any type of limited drinking is that someday, somewhere, sometime, something is going to happen to justify raising your limit, and then everything changes. The first change is to the thinking or reasoning that caused you to set a limit for yourself in the first place. Someone like this has probably developed a tolerance to alcohol because of his or her routine over a period of time. The impact of another drink may have the effect of six more drinks! As time goes by, one's tolerance can go down, and the effects of drinking your limit will be greater on you at some point in the future. If you do not know what will happen then, there is reason to be concerned.

Also, if you constantly have alcohol in your system, you will risk it interacting with any other prescription or over-the-counter drug you take. The resulting combined effects are chemically incalculable, and the outcome would only be a SWAG (sophisticated wild-ass guess). Mixing drugs, including the drug alcohol, can be fatal, and no one should experiment with this! My answer then becomes open-ended, because any little change in the equation will change the outcome. You would be better served by trying to skip some days in between drinking and observing whether or not you are physically uncomfortable with this new drinking schedule.

2. "Why should I be interested in the AA program? I have heard lots of drinking stories and I am not that bad."

Alcoholism is like an elevator that you can get off of near the top floor, or you can ride that baby right into the cellar. When do you think it's best for you?

How many negative results are needed in your life to convince you there might be a better way of life by taking a different road rather than getting another shaft?

I've never seen AA harm someone, but I have seen alcohol kill people who were still on the elevator. There are many things that can happen to drunks from which there is no return or no amends. We read about these unfortunate events every day, and we are often misled by obituaries that are written to protect the families of accidental or suicidal overdoses. The public is therefore misinformed as to the extent that drugs and alcohol affect their lives and their communities.

I recently attended an AA meeting where a father of a twenty-three-year-old girl, who had been killed by a drunk driver, was present. The father remains active in the fellowship to maintain his personal sobriety and sanity.

During this meeting, I could not help but think of the day when that driver might walk through the same door and ask for help with his drinking problem and in putting his life back in order. I choose to believe that AA would find a way to help them both live beyond this avoidable tragedy. In the end, you are the judge, and nothing good can come of any of this, unless you decide the AA program and fellowship is for you.

3. "What will happen if I stop drinking for a few months and then return when I feel better?"

This is easy. First, you can refer to question number two above. Then, you get back on the elevator, but not on the same floor you got off. The known history of the progression of alcoholism tells us that it will continue even after you stop drinking.

Therefore, you will get back on the elevator a few floors closer to the cellar and continue your ride. If you attend AA meetings for those few months, your outlook will be completely different. Your decision might be in favor of a better life with hope, understanding, and love. This would be a perfect opportunity for you to check out AA and see if anything connects for you in the rooms. If it is not for you, we will refund all of your problems when you leave. The program is only for those who want it, not need it. You get to choose. We only advise and caution.

4. "Why should I stop drinking when my only problems were DUI's, and now I always arrange for a ride or call a cab?"

A long history of DUI's is the greatest predictor of more DUI's, or even worse things like a crash, injury, or a death. Let's say if you had three DUI's, you probably drove drunk forty or fifty times—or more! (You won't convince me otherwise. Been there, done that, skipped the t-shirt.) I worry about limits, promises, and plans made, because your thinking changes the more you drink and/or the longer you drink. Alcoholism is an insidious disease that will misinform you about yourself and your apparent capabilities. It will help you make bad decisions.

This is a scary scenario for me, and I have to suggest a different way of life before something happens that you cannot correct. Remember "what causes a problem is the problem", and in this case I think that you have addressed the wrong issue. If you want to forget about the police, judges, lawyers, costs, fees, points on your license, increases in your insurance (if you still have it), and classes put on by the DMV, then I would suggest a meeting to address the real problem, which is your drinking, not your driving. DMV will also insist on a professional evaluation by a counselor, and if you answer those questions honestly you will probably end up in rehabilitation or mandated to AA meetings for a designated period. In addition, new and exciting issues will soon become apparent, making this an inappropriate question in the first place.

5. "Why does my husband choose drinking over his family responsibilities?"

Because he *can't not* make those decisions. Rough grammatically, but I hope you get the point. Alcohol-affected decisions are not clear intelligent choices made based on current input of information, logic, history, or even morals. They are literally drug-affected and blurred or distorted beyond normal reason. If you press an active alcoholic for an answer, all you will get is what you want to hear. You have to remove the alcohol from the alcoholic before you can pose serious questions concerning his or her actions, if you want to deal in reality and feel comfortable with the decisions that are reached. Amateurs dealing with drinkers are destined to make mistakes without the help of a sober member of the AA program or a professional to guide them. The power of addiction is a formidable force, and you may need lots of help trying to get someone turned around. There is nothing unusual about this, so reach out and ask for personal help.

6. "How much time will I need to devote to meetings?"

I always recommend you devote almost as much time to meetings that you gave to drinking in the beginning. After you get a good footing, you can begin to substitute other healthy activities, while keeping up a good amount of time in the rooms.

Ninety meetings in ninety days are usually recommended, plus or minus given the individual's life schedule, but only approached on a one-day-at-a-time basis. Time is your friend here, so try to remember that you didn't get into this mess overnight, and the importance of sobriety and your growth in the program deserves a fair portion of your time now. There is no express degree available, the elevator is broken, and the steps take some time. The more you invest of yourself, the greater the personal return. Don't cheat yourself. You will find that meetings are a sanctuary for those who seek help. The fellowship and understanding you will find there will draw you in. This is a really good thing!

7. "If I go to a rehabilitation facility to get started, what effect will it have on my job?

Alcoholism is widely accepted as a disease, and your employer should act as if you were out for treatment for any kind of disease. He or she should also allow flexibility in your work schedule when you return to aid in keeping your treatment plan and meetings in good order. Your boss will probably be happy because your future work with them will improve in terms of attendance, reliability, and overall work performance. They're not dumb. Employers know why you feel like crap every morning and are distracted from fully focusing on your job. Ask yourself how many other coworkers are always running late on Monday mornings and after lunch breaks, frequently don't feel well, and sometimes smell funny. The cost of repairing you is far smaller than the cost of recruiting, training, and replacing you with an unknown. They will be happy in helping you become more productive and more valuable as an employee to them. Besides, no one likes to let someone go when they know full well that the problem is correctable. For your information, if you do not drink or smoke, you can smell someone who does from across a large room. Your secret concerns about your drinking are usually well known by most of the people around you. If you think this is a big secret, you need to get a clue.

Remember that only ten percent of the population drinks problematically, so the other ninety percent have already sniffed you out! Relax and try not to create roadblocks to success.

8. "Can I still visit my friends in the bars after I stop drinking?"

Sure; let me load the gun for you, because you are about to shoot yourself in the foot! It should be years before you are comfortable to safely visit a bar, and even then I would question your reasoning. No matter how strong you are, the chances of this scenario becoming a train wreck are overwhelming, especially over time.

I have a close friend in the fellowship that likes to say: "If you hang around a barber shop long enough, you're going to get a hair cut!" You would be far better off to wait for your friends to bump into you at a meeting, if they remember you at all two days after you stop going into those bars.

Barroom friendships were the most shallow and meaningless relationships available to me. You deserve better, and the program will reward you for practicing the principles in all of your affairs. Even today, some thirty-plus years later, when my wife wants to go to some family affair that involves drinking, I stay home and babysit our cat. Real friends and relatives will understand that there will be another, more appropriate time to get together when we can all feel good about it.

Watching people deteriorate while drinking is no longer any fun to me and serves no useful purpose in my sober life, and besides, they can get over it! This is my life.

9. "I always felt at ease while drinking and it helped me to be more sociable. What's going to happen after I stop drinking?"

You will undoubtedly experience some difficulties, and you may even want to seek specialized help to guide you through these personal problems. I would suggest that you try to table these issues for a while for two reasons: One, time will help you adjust naturally. And two, the longer you can wait, the more sobriety will help you find some solutions on your own. You are going to feel uncomfortable about a lot of things, but this is the way we learn to cope in the real world. You will gain experience and work through situations, so long as you don't drink and go to meetings. As time goes by, you will probably begin to feel more and enjoy more.

Life wasn't designed to be lived under the influence of alcohol, and the sober appreciation of life and all it feels like will fill your life as soon as you get a grip on sobriety.

10. "What do you mean when you say 'blackout'?"

In layman terms, a blackout is a period of time lost by your memory, during which you have been functioning "normally" after drinking enough to cause your memory to stop working. People continue to drink, eat, party, talk, drive, and engage in any number of social intercourses while appearing to be under the influence of alcohol, but otherwise acting rather normal. These periods are usually recognized by problem drinkers who awake and cannot remember leaving their drinking location, getting home, or anything in between. This can be a scary time, or an easy way to "write off" whatever you did or said during the blackout that others will probably point out to you on your next visit with them. Blackouts are therefore one of the biggest reasons that people begin to wonder if they might need help of some sort.

A problem drinker can be recognized by often denying that he or she has not done something recalled to them after a blackout. This is a common problem in the world of drinking to varying degrees, and normally becomes progressively worse with continued heavy drinking or the gradual loss of normal tolerances to drinking. An active sign of a blackout in progress is when you hear someone who has been drinking tell the same exact story over and over again, even using the same words! They do not remember a few moments ago, and will not remember their repetitions the next day.

One of the inspired features of the AA program is the availability of discussion meetings held throughout the network of local chapters and groups. At these meetings, subjects often formed by questions like those above, or current concerns of a member, can be the focus of a particular meeting and the collective experience of the members gathered can be tapped into. Each member is usually given a reasonable period of time to speak briefly on the chosen topic. In this way, you can learn how different folks may correctly respond and share their experience and opinions, in an effort to find the right and meaningful answer for you. My answers above are an example of what I would say at that meeting, and of course, you would hear other responses from those gathered for the same meeting.

One of the mysteries of AA is that you may hear a similar answer from a different personality, and it will suddenly make sense to you and become a valuable part of your personal recovery. All this helps define the purpose of AA by way of people helping people in an effort to maintain their own sobriety. If you can go home at the end of the day feeling you helped someone else stay sober, you insure another day sober for yourself. Attending meetings creates its own rewards.

The founders of this program were simple people who collectively designed a program and fellowship to stay sober that is now seen as pure genius. All you have to do is go to meetings and let the program sink in. You and your family deserve nothing less.

CHAPTER 8

Experience Demonstrates Alcoholism is Insidious, Treacherous, and Patient

Alcoholism is a progressive disease. Once it gets a hold of you, it will never change course; it will only progress. I don't know if it takes root at or before the first drink, or somewhere along the way, but if you have problems with your drinking, then you are going to encounter progression. I have seen and personally experienced strong-willed people try to limit their drinking in order to curtail the problems that crept into their lives, only to see failure time and time again.

Alcoholism is therefore also possessive, as it does not want to let anyone go easily.

Getting yourself straight is never an easy task, but you can find plenty of help at the meetings of Alcoholics Anonymous.

"Man takes a drink, the drink takes a drink, and then the drink takes the man!"

I remember as far back as fifty years ago when my grandfather drank one large bottle of beer after work every day and had no problem, until he would drink just one more and go off the deep end. My father would make himself a perfect Manhattan and sip it all night long, also with no problem. He would sometimes offer my grandfather a sample, only to see him belt it down like a short beer! The effects were visible, and it would irk my father to no end. Also, each year during my grandfather's company picnics, he would add to his limited drinking and would arrive home in a heap. I doubt that he was an alcoholic in the classic sense, but the mystery of alcohol was there and has become memorable over all these years. I mention this to illustrate that any change in one's routine is likely to blow out one's original plan and create negative results. Therefore, the unexpected should be expected, as long as you understand progression and the power of alcohol.

There have been many times of trying various limits as a method to control my drinking that would fail for me because some minor event or the timing would encourage another drink. That's the drink taking a drink! I would start drinking, knowing I had limited time and impending obligations, only to find myself making excuses to have another drink. Then the telephone calls would start— to cover my time and extend my schedule— in order to drink some more. That's the drink taking the man! I would then blow off the day, and when I felt filled by my drinking, I would head for home to sleep it off. Those trips home were rarely completed without another stop at another bar along the way. This didn't happen once; it happened all the time, and with increasing problems on the other side. Just about everyone's vision of me was that of a nicely dressed successful salesman with not a care in the world, because I led two lives by separating myself from most people when it was time for me to drink. I could not face those close to me, as I feared ridicule or questions about why I drank the way I drank.

There are countless examples of this adage at work with alcoholics, and it is relentless. Even if one is successful in maintaining their limits as time goes by, their tolerance wanes. <u>As the tolerance goes down, the effect produced by the alcohol goes up!</u> When the effect goes up, your adherence to your own controls goes out the window, and off you go! Alcohol is insidious, treacherous, and patient. It is pure insanity if you think you can find a way around this truth. Do you remember when you first learned how to conjugate the word drink (drink, drank, drunk)? As an alcoholic, all I need to do is drink and I am drunk.

The "ism" in alcoholism alters my mind and expedites the effects of anything I might drink to my brain. There is no time left for "drank". The most valuable lesson learned here is: it's the first drink that gets you drunk! This also demonstrates why surrender is necessary when battling alcoholism. We cannot afford even one drink. Sorry.

Even when you may stop drinking all together for a time (any time), the progression is still advancing within you. If and when you return to drinking, you will quickly realize that time has not stopped, and the effects alcohol have on you are at the least the same, or more likely, worse than before. Statistically, only about fifty percent of new arrivals to AA who really try to get the program will succeed on the first try. The balance will have to continue to try again and again. AA suggests that only half of that segment will succeed after several tries, bringing the hopeful success rate to seventy-five percent. The balance will have to prove this to themselves, and hopefully they will return to AA when they are more ready. So, the industrious drinker comes up with some different limits, different times, different concoctions, different places, etc. The results will also be different. They will be worse. Progression is inescapable, and if you argue this point you are in denial and seriously damaged by your drinking (to be kind). It would be best to find a meeting and/ or some professional help. Why try to come up with a new and exciting plan that will put you in the last twenty-five percent of alcoholics who will probably die alcoholically? Why not surrender and let God sort it all out?

At the lowest times in my life that are too ugly to write about, I didn't think things could get worse for me, but they always did. Alcohol wasn't the second love of my life; it controlled my life; it dictated what I would say, what I would do, and where I would go. New lower horizons would emerge and drag me along. Deeper and deeper into the progression of alcoholism, I watched my life unravel and deteriorate by the day. Many people can say they *aren't that bad yet* as an excuse, but they will be if they can live long enough.

The question becomes whether or not they can literally survive the alcoholic poisoning and physical dangers that loom in the darkness of this level of addiction. You have to be pretty stubborn and strong to have even a small chance to find the end of this rope, while thinking that everything is okay because you have enough money for your next drink. Enough to get a tab started in the lowest of the bars in town, enough to play pool to win for some drinks, or to prolong your visit in a dive long enough to talk someone into "loaning" you money until whenever. Other drunks will understand and try to help so you can continue drinking and deteriorating mentally and physically. Spirituality has usually slipped away by the time these events fill your day.

Progression makes you think that the circumstances such as those above are acceptable because you are still drinking and not feeling much. The longer one stays in this low stage of life, the greater the excuses become to justify your existence there and postpone doing something constructive about it. Everyone's Bowery is located somewhere different. You don't have to go there; it comes to you.

It finds you. When you are in the deepest of ruts, you cannot imagine being able to climb out to a better life. That time has past. You feel you are predestined. This is what you deserve. Normal, hopeful thinking is not possible when your brain is so affected by alcohol, because it is a seriously depressive drug you can take without limits, coupled with the damage being done to the brain cells by the drug alcohol itself. So even when the writing is on the wall, you just can't read it! Your brain is wired differently now; thinking is sporadic, uncertain, unreliable.

Active drunks cannot usually process information on the spot, so the only mission here is to get them dried out some way or another. Then, you can talk to them in hopes of guiding them toward a better life plan. Don't give up on them; they are still part of your life, part of your love. It is possible to return to a real life.

An active drinker is actively producing excuses to protect his or her right to drink and will hear little or nothing, no matter how well meaning you are. So, dry them out now, talk later. AA is patient, too.

An often heard topic in the rooms is progression, and any new guy or gal will hear many stories they can relate to if they attend enough meetings early on.

Hearing of similar personal exploits from others promotes understanding and the ability to relate to someone who is admitting he or she is an alcoholic—part of the first step. This will help solidify the whole reason he or she is here in the meeting. Everyone is affected by this phenomenon, so it is truly universal, and the testimonies heard will grind these truths into anyone over time. Once you dry out and have admitted your lack of manageability in your life, your next mission is to shut up for awhile and listen to things like this, so you can find you own way out of the mess you drank yourself into. You are no longer alone! You are not different!

You are one of us.

If you think you are "not as bad" as a speaker, then you are not. But you *are* destined to find new lows as they lurk around the next corner for any alcoholic who cannot stop drinking. If you are lucky enough to stay alive long enough, you will dig an even deeper rut to live in. I finally elected to let the people who went lower that I win that contest. That became a part of my surrender in order to find a better life, and for me, there was nowhere else to go but up. I did not say that I couldn't write about my lowest times for some kind of drama, I said it because it is stuff that is too ugly, too dirty, and disgusting to repeat. I had to stop drinking and start changing or I would have died. It is only when you can let go of your old defenses that you will get the opportunity to fall into a softer place. It won't happen quickly every time, but it won't hurt as much as the crap you have been putting yourself through. Try it; your life may be in the balance.

Attitude is everything in recovery. You have to keep your attitude in check every day if you are serious about staying sober. Let me approach this from the dark side! Everyone, everywhere, every time says the same two words just before picking up a drink again. Can you guess which two words they are? "Fuck it!" Those are the words of surrender to an outside source or other challenge to the manner in which we are trying to live our lives sober. We are giving up for some reason. Something in our lives is going wrong, and for some reason, we are not respecting all we have learned in the meetings, or we suddenly disbelieve the tenets that have provided us with a better way of living.

You have to stop and think about all the good things sobriety has brought you already. How do you feel right now compared to how you felt when you were completely out of control? Do you feel better? Do you think better? Lord knows, you have been acting better! What about the people in your life who again have begun to trust you and depend on you to be doing the right things. Do you suddenly think you can drink safely after the hundreds of times you have proven that wrong? You need to get real and get over the "Fuck it!" urge. Don't let your attitude defeat you in the greatest mission you have ever tackled.

When you have issues about something that is going on in your life that brings you to a point just before those famous two works kick in, then you need to get honest with yourself and open up to someone about your concerns. You have arrived at this point by stuffing your feelings, and now it is time to reverse that thinking. The first thing you probably need is a meeting, a call to your sponsor, or some sort of impromptu meeting with a fellow alcoholic in recovery. Get yourself in front of someone who gives a shit about you and spill your guts! Tell someone you are about to ruin your life all over again and you need his or her help—NOW! No one will put you off, and you can forget feeling like this has never happened to anyone else in the program, because it has happened to all of us at one time or another. This is the critical point that separates the winners from the losers. The winners reach out and give the program a chance to kick in. You do not have to drink! The only difference here is the outcome, based on the plan of action taken when these times arise for each of us. If you reach out, a hand will be there.

You need to position yourself to succeed at these times by gathering and remembering the information you have heard in the various meetings. This stuff is your lifeline, and you must be connected to survive. If you drink, you may never get back to us.

How well prepared you are and how successful you have been in gathering the many help lines available throughout the fellowship will ultimately define the outcome of your problem and how you handle it. If you isolate, you are on your own. If you reach out, we can help. Facing this current issue will be easier than juggling the massive problems that will follow your return to active drinking. If you have suddenly decided that are "not that bad yet," then you have to figure out just how bad you are going to have to be before you can admit this program was designed with you in mind. Remember the elevator ride. You got off the elevator, and now you are thinking it is somehow okay to jump back on and see just how deep you can go. Newsflash: The elevator does not have an up button! Some would tell you simply to use the "steps".

The whole reason for writing this book was for me to try to keep people off the damn elevator! You have to learn to let all the horror stories you've heard satisfy your need to explore the depths of alcoholism. Recovering alcoholics do not need any horror stories because someone is having trouble surrendering him or herself to this simple program. Give yourself another day without drinking, go to a meeting, and things will improve without further research on the elevator.

Unfortunately, a lot of the people who insist on continuing their ride on the elevator will never know what hit them when the next disaster strikes. You read about these people often. To endanger yourself or others is purely foolish after the members of AA and the literature available in their rooms have educated you. The excuses are gone! You are now responsible for yourself again because you are sober. You are making these kinds of decisions fully armed with education about your condition. Experts are counseling you. People who really know. People who really care.

When someone who has two or three times the legal limit of alcohol in their system and decides to drive, it is understandable to me because they could not have made a good decision if their life depended on it. For you to take a drink again now condones that kind of decision in advance, which is neither understandable nor defensible. Let me simplify this. It's *stupid!*

The great majority of the members of your community are on the side of your continuing sobriety. They admire your commitment to improve yourself, and I am sure they feel safer because of your current actions. An abrupt return to drinking can also lead to an accidental overdose with dire results. What makes you think you can control this? Once you drink, the problem drinker is not making the decisions, the drink is! Are you prepared to accept the outcome of a drink's decision? Are you willing to pay with your time—or your life?

Not everyone understands AA, especially non-members, but I have never been heckled at a meeting in a church building or when sitting at a diner having coffee with the most important people in my life. AA is like a family and without them, other family relationships would suffer, if not disintegrate. Do yourself a favor and seek out a solution to the things that bother you now, rather than create new problems that may not have a solution. Staying sober, one day at a time, sometimes one hour at a time, is challenging, but it is doable.

When someone finally succeeds in getting sober it is still a one-day-at-a-time adventure. Each new day presents challenges, questions, and rewards we are better able to recognize, process, and/or enjoy. This is a basic topic, but it enjoys many a discussion in the rooms because it is so important and diverse. I am sure that everyone will bring new and exciting experiences with them as they progress in the program and the many meetings they will gratefully attend in the fellowship.

If I was asked to conjugate the word drink now, I would say, "Drink, drunk, dead!" The day I wrote this chapter, a member of my AA home group was found dead in an apartment.

He was fifty-five years old. He was having trouble staying sober. He had moved a few miles away from the people who could have saved his life. If you don't reach out for help, it doesn't matter if your overdose was accidental or suicidal. You are still dead. This is not a story. This really happened in Saratoga Springs, New York, on April 30, 2009. Who do you think will be next? I can only guess that it will not be someone I see every day in a meeting, really trying to help him or herself. They are keeping themselves in position to be able to reach out and ask for help when it is needed.

"The people I see in meetings are the people I see in meetings!" When you establish a pattern of making meetings and trying to progress, you will, and you have a far better chance to live beyond alcoholism. These things are freely given, but must be accepted when you are serious about getting better.

CHAPTER 9

Adjusting to Sobriety

My personal experience was enhanced by some medical problems, as the title suggests, but I think anyone who survives alcoholism would be well served to consider him or herself on borrowed time. No one is capable of predicting the outcome of any particular drinking adventure when personal control has been lost for some time. When drinking is restarted, I would be careful in predicting safe and healthy endings after addiction has been displayed.

Progression will sneak up on problem drinkers and change the impact on them without prior announcement, and the mental impact will completely alter their way of thinking. Adding a drink to one's usual amount of consumption can multiply the effects, not just change them a little. Decisions are then drug-affected. Outcomes are so unpredictable because of the progression that may exist within one's drinking experience given the amount of time spent in trying to medicate one's feelings, one drink at a time, over years. To have reached this level of concern in recovery is worthy of celebration because of the sobriety achieved in the process of trying to improve your way of life. But this is where the one-day-at-a-time concept so importantly comes into play.

Our success is only as good as our ability to continue our plans of sobriety, and that requires vigilance, stamina, and clear thinking. Priority one is to *not drink and go to a meeting!* If that doesn't work for you, *go to a meeting and don't drink!* When you start each day with those thoughts, you are at least headed in the right direction. Even if you have concerns on your mind, getting together with others in the process of recovery will bring you to a good place mentally. It will change your outlook on life. At the meeting, you can ask questions without judgment and soak up advice and experience you didn't have to pay for. Before you leave the meeting, resolve not to drink, and have a plan about where and when your next meeting will be. If you bury your concerns and avoid meetings, you will only succeed in isolating yourself from meaningful support and encouragement when it is most needed. When you stuff your feelings, you are getting ready to drink again, so open up and start to work things out. You owe it to yourself.

Don't let your ego get in the way of sobriety. If you feel embarrassed about some event or thought, you haven't heard anything yet! You are now in association with people who could make your hair curl with their own stories, if you give them the time and opportunity to share with you. You can also rely on your sponsor in an effort to keep things private. *Nobody ever got sober alone!* You have to open up and let other people know what you are thinking and feeling. To maintain your stamina, you should be aware of your diet, exercise, and sleep patterns to promote a healthy style of living and to feel good about yourself. When you feel good it is easier to make good decisions. In recovery, clear thinking is first maintained by not drinking and is usually further defined by the amount of time you have had away from your last drink. This is especially true in early recovery. It takes a serious amount of time for the fog to clear, sometimes years . . . so remember that your depth of understanding will change as time passes and you begin to get better.

Sobriety is an adventure you actually remember! I can quickly recall the many times I was winging it while suffering from a devastating hangover or blackout issues at my work. People I did not remember would approach me and ask if their car was ready for delivery, as I have mentioned before. The effects of the blackouts had begun to occur, and damaged brain cells are not resilient. Once you kill off a large number of cells with excessive drinking, they will remain dead and will affect your memory in increasingly scary ways for many years to come. Having clear memory now is truly a benefit worth celebrating when I consider just how far I could have gone while protecting my right to drink. Today, my ability to remember improves constantly, given my age, as I have added quite a few years to my sobriety and now really enjoy the many aspects of living sober and fully enjoying life. Time heals.

Focusing on things one day at a time is as simplistic as it sounds. The bold reality is that it is impossible to live any other way. For me, this suggestion keeps me focused on today, rather than worrying about yesterday's concerns or tomorrow's possible problems. If you try to live those three days at the same time, there is no way you can be clear in your thinking or in your actions. There is no good reason to complicate your sobriety plan by getting distracted because your thinking is scattered about on too many things. Live in the moment, and enjoy the blessings that will find you without your trying. Keep your priorities straight. *Staying sober is first!* Everything else has to take a back seat for a while and be handled when you are ready, willing, and able to address the other issues.

This does not mean you can be selfish, but that you must remain realistic about what you can handle right now. It probably took the better part of a lifetime to get into this mess, so don't expect smooth sailing in a matter of weeks or months. Make sure you respect how others feel about you first, because your memory is not only one-dimensional, it is probably foggy at best. Give everyone a chance to air his or her thoughts before you charge ahead. If you find a day at a time is too long a period to handle early on, break it down to half a day, or an hour at a time! Just hold on so progress can continue because of your efforts already invested in forming a new way of life. Be patient with yourself.

When you finally realize staying stopped is easier for you than starting and stopping drinking again and again, then you have reached a critical point in your recovery. No one wants to admit that their drinking and life are unmanageable, or that they are—heaven forbid—addicted. Meanwhile, you have been demonstrating just that to yourself at the same time you have been trying to figure out why you have so many life problems. Staying stopped is critical to your recovery.

This was one of my favorite justifications to restart drinking after being introduced to AA. First, I convinced myself that one drink never hurt anyone, not even a child. In fact, it probably helped everyone (remember that only ten percent of people drink problematically). Then, I would stop at my local watering spot after work for one drink and go home sober, proving I was right. The next day I would stop again and end up having a second drink to congratulate myself on proving my theory and go home sober yet again. The third day I got drunk! The next day I would have trouble stopping my drinking because the addiction had taken hold of me again! *You do not need to try this!* Let me be the last blazing idiot to attempt overcoming alcoholism with such an uninformed plan.

Any form or amount of alcohol is a mind-altering drug that has only one mission: to alter your thinking. Once you have allowed the start of the process by taking a drink, the addiction takes over your thinking. Now, in fact, you cannot remember how you reached the conclusion that one drink never hurt anyone. The insidiousness of alcoholism makes you try to think of more ways to justify another plan supporting drinking, rather than stopping, because now it is easier to drink than to stop again. This type of thinking is what prolongs the misery of alcoholism, and it is self-perpetuating. One has to look back soberly to when you realized that staying stopped is easier to live with and success will appear to you.

Experience will also demonstrate that the longer you can stay stopped, the better you feel about all aspects of your life. The physical habit of drinking can be changed with amazing results in the way you think, feel, and act. Most importantly, you will regain control of how you think! Why should we allow some substance to control the way we think? Most of my feelings were shrouded by alcohol, and many of my actions were deplorable under the influence of alcohol. It is hard to explain why we continue to try to find ways to justify drinking while we are amassing a history of unexplainable feelings and creating an even longer list of actions we may well regret the rest of our lives. At some point in our history, we have to accept the responsibility that our lives are no longer manageable, and that the lack of manageability permeated our lives because of our addiction to alcohol. *Alcohol influenced us.* Those circumstances negatively altered our own lives and the lives of those around us until we found a way to stay stopped. Stop the *vicious* cycle. Begin to live again.

I find myself questioning the often-heard statement: "I understand." When I hear this, I always wonder what it really means. Does that person have complete depth of understanding of that particular subject? Has he exhausted all sources of information on the topic and, most importantly to me, has he lived a life that included some personal experience that confirmed his findings? Part of my answer would be that if he is a member of AA and the topic has anything to do with any aspect of alcoholism and living in sobriety, he is probably at least on the right track. The other part of my answer would be that I doubt most everyone else. My point is that people in AA delve into life, and their understandings are well researched and thought out. Proven by experience. Understanding comes in degrees. Like any endeavor, you need to really feel the need to know and be fueled by a passion that will drive you to a full and complete conclusion. Peeling back the first layer of an onion does not allow the conclusion that it is not rotten at the core. This is just the beginning of the evidence that will lead you to an understanding, a new knowledge. Taking a big bite of it would also add real experience to your evaluation but may end up being the tearful approach. This is an example of why I think AA is helpful to everyone. They are all willing to share their experiences, strengths, and hopes to help educate and guide newer people who have limited experience in the many topics that will concern them as they try to get and stay sober. AA is a journey with many destinations and no real end, except for the end of life experience that you have finally overcome the effects of alcoholism through the use of the fellowship. The members will help you peel back the layers of life and find the deepest and truest of understandings needed to adjust your way of living and growth in sobriety. By giving back to new members, we stay sober.

Relationships. When at last we begin sobering up, some of the first pains felt are the pains of loneliness created by our recent manner of living. Alcoholism, in and of itself, is a cruel assault on our loved ones that they didn't bargain for. More often than not, we find ourselves alone or estranged from our loved ones, at least temporarily. As we begin to feel better physically, spiritually, and mentally, we also find ourselves feeling an emptiness that hurts from deep within. Our natural reaction is to reach out for companionship to soothe those feelings. In recovery, we have to keep our priorities in line. Recovery is first and foremost, and relationships should be tabled for at least one year. I know we all want reinforcement and acceptance by others, and that is healthy, as long as you leave it in the rooms of AA.

Besides, the closeness of our new friends may unreasonably trump the frayed relationships that belonged to us prior to seeking help. If given a reasonable amount of time, about a year or so, our former relationships may mend and improve, so returning to our core families is a viable option that does not need to be compromised by a new relationship. It is infinitely easier to start a new relationship than to repair an old one, but the old one deserves your efforts and amends more that you need to experiment and try to make yourself feel better. When you research this, you will understand.

Finances. I suppose some people can skip this subject, but every time I fetched up in treatment and recovery, my finances were usually nil. In early recovery, we have to keep a lid on the importance of our finances because, again, we have to maintain our priorities. As you begin to progress into a recovery that may involve rehabilitation facilities, halfway houses, AA meetings, and new beginnings in the real world, your focus should be on just having enough for now. Getting back to the old job or seeking a new and rewarding career are good things to be planning for, rather than acting on. Simplicity in our way of life and having a schedule are important to improve confidence in building a new way of life in sobriety. Rushing into new and challenging opportunities distracts our focus from learning how to be sober first. Adding time to sobriety will allow us to learn from the meetings and add to the most important job of finding people with similar experiences that we can identify with and rely on. *Easy does it!* Stability is more important than changing the world today. Give time that is needed to logically grow slowly and firmly in a sober way of life. Pay attention to the basics of life, and in time you will better understand.

Health. Regardless of your age, you will probably find yourself at another turning point once you start trying to get sober. Diet and exercise have not been high on a drinker's list of things to be concerned about, let alone seeing a doctor on any kind of a routine schedule. Historically, we have not thought about ourselves and have not cared for ourselves as a result. You will be best served to find a doctor and tell him you have started to get sober and want his or her advice, a physical, and appropriate tests to determine a proper diet and exercise program, or possible medical or psychological treatment plan. *This decision could save your life.* Most drinkers have neglected themselves physically because of their soggy thinking and mental depression caused by alcohol. It could be months before you begin to feel what is really going on inside yourself, so don't try to diagnose yourself. Leave it to the professionals, and you may well be surprised by the results of this type of examination. You will not be successful getting sober if you overlook a physical illness that needs immediate treatment or one that may cause you to suffer from a deep clinical depression that will impede your future progress in sobriety.

We have to address all concerns to insure success. I know today that had I not sobered up when I did, I could not have survived the physical challenges that lurked around the very next corner of my life. I always felt fine or made excuses for not feeling fine before I got sober. I may have easily made the wrong choices, or been in the wrong state of mind, when my first heart attack started. Had I not been in control of my life through sobriety, my life would have simply ended in July 1998. That is the bold truth! Because I held on to the basics of the AA program and progressed normally beyond my drinking days, I was better able to understand and act appropriately, seeking emergency medical assistance right away. Sobriety also added to my stamina helping me to endure the physical challenges, various medical treatments, and procedures ahead.

I hope I have not ruined the word "understanding" for you, but I think it critical to realize the depth of any such understanding when it comes to subjects that are of life and death importance. Your grasp of the proper concepts promoted by Alcoholics Anonymous is of the greatest importance. Not only is your life on the line, but also those who love you deserve your best effort in growing in sobriety, so they can reasonably expect you to return their love by the way you live your life now and in the future. The average drunk, and I doubt that you are unusual, has left a wake of destruction behind him or her and some of those problems may not quickly surface or be readily resolved. You need to find that passion I talk about that will drive you to dig deeply into AA and life, by searching out all the information you need to get sober and stay sober. The level of your understanding will determine the success you have living sober and being able to make amends to those in your personal wake who deserve it. Never take lightly the depth and reality of your understanding in and of your sobriety.

CHAPTER 10

A Look at Feelings From an Alcoholic Point of View

Active alcoholism will take you to places you did not plan to go. Some of the most hurtful places are deep within your own body and mind. Addiction takes you without asking. You go there because you must. You are not at the controls anymore. When you resist, multiple feelings will result, making the journey more difficult, the destination more uncertain. If you have reason to be concerned about your drinking behaviors, you will probably recognize some, if not all, of the following feelings I experienced while protecting my right to drink. I did not know I was on an elevator and that I could get off at any floor. I thought continued drinking would be the solution to my problems. Feelings can be experienced in many ways; most of them I found to be extremely painful even though I was usually under the influence of alcohol. Sedated, but not enough . . .

Love. A deep and fond memory of love always smoldered from within. When I reached out during my drinking times, I was usually disappointed with the results, unless it was late and my vision and sense of right and wrong were distorted. Love is the fuel that causes our hearts to beat and push blood throughout our bodies, always wanting, never reliable. Love usually brought tears to my eyes as I remembered my past, my loves, family, and children. The memories were there to tantalize me and cause me to fantasize, because the further I got away from real love, the more I wanted it. Love is the most basic of emotions, but alcohol trumped it with me. Alcohol overshadowed everything and caused a distortion of love and all feelings in order to remain in control of my life.

When I would clearly see the absence of real love in my life, my thoughts and feelings would change to hate.

Hate. No one understood me! They did not really know what was going on in my life. Their dark looks and shrugs showed me their disdain and outward feelings about me. I would want to fight back and show them. I hated the so-called normal people around me. Who were they? What gave them the right to judge me? Even my dislikes would always grow into hating as the alcohol I was drinking wore away at my inhibitions, my intellect. Hate caused me to disregard my own personal safety in situations that had little to do with anyone except myself. Were the thoughts of suicide creeping nearer to my present? Would continued drinking pause those thoughts or hasten them? Hate was what I felt for myself. It often seemed there was nothing else left for me except to hate and be hated. Hate closed my world around me, trying to snuff out the smoldering of any love left within.

Anguish. That feeling of uselessness and inner commotion crippled me. The absence of manageability in my life pulled and pushed me according to feelings I could no longer control. My heart would tell me one thing, my head another, my gut something all together different. Which way should I go? When I would try to figure this out, all the feelings would change and confuse me. A clear decision was not possible; my actions frozen in fear of doing the wrong thing . . . again. These confusions would endure and multiply, twisting me from within somewhere. Surely another drink would help me sort this out. How foolish.

Disappointment. I felt this about so many things and people, but my biggest disappointment was myself. Every time I would try to accomplish something, I would fall short because I could not follow through. I was always distracted by the need to drink, and my need to drink was the strongest of feelings. Without alcohol in my system, I could not think clearly. I could not decide. I could not justify anything. All roads led me toward another drink or the plan of another drink as soon as possible. I could not lose touch with the flow of booze that soothed my gut, quieted my head, and excited me as a man. Whatever I wanted to think about, drinking would permeate my plans, demanding to be a part of everything and causing me to be disappointed in my lack of control. The longer I would deny myself of drinking, the greater the physical and mental facets of my being would scream out, demanding more alcohol, or I would feel like I was coming apart from the inside out. Disappointment is what I felt. Addiction is what I was living.

Lust. In the beginning of my drinking, the early beginning, alcohol would soothe my nerves and give me courage to reach out socially and sexually. I was a teenager with no experience. It took the edge off of my hesitations, telling me all was well and I could really do anything and it would turn out okay. While urging me forward, alcohol caused me to make excuses for anything that I came across that made me think I should not proceed. My increasing lust made anything acceptable. As time went by, this would turn on me and cause me to feel lust simply because I was drinking. *Then I would want to drink just to feel lust!* This vicious cycle got its start in my teen years and would progress over the years of problem drinking and keep me on the edge of trouble many, many times. These feelings would come back to haunt me many years later, in different ways, almost as if to punish me. Full memories were rarely available to me as I searched for things I needed to make amends for. I began to realize some of the worst wrongs I had done over the many years would go undisclosed and unamended. It was lust that dropped this on the doorstep of my personal recovery. I would have to learn to cope, and to justify where necessary, in order to get through the steps and begin to heal.

Greed. I developed a feeling of entitlement in order to justify all of my decisions to continue drinking rather than to engage in responsible thinking. When you repeatedly favor anything that allows continued drinking, you devalue any alternative on the table. I never had trouble spending the vast majority of my money on drinking and drinking activities while stepping over any other obligation I was responsible for. If my ex-wife needed money for rent, I knew the landlord would hold off. If my landlord wanted his money, I knew he would stand a better chance to recover his money if he let me stay, rather than throw me out and take his losses. If my children needed food and supplies, I knew their grandparents would intervene to save the day. I would make promises and sometimes actually pay some of what I owed, but nothing got paid if it meant I had to stop drinking. If I was able to keep the flow of alcohol going, I would not have to feel the outcome of my actions. My personal greed would always prevail.

Sloth or laziness. As I would sit and just drink, my whole being would adjust to accommodate drinking. My hunger did not exist. My ambitions would subside or become a story to tell at the bar. My goals put on hold. My plans going out of focus. Drinking and the resulting feelings caused by drinking were the most important things going on. Drinking made me approve of more drinking, because if some was good, more would be better! If work obligations haunted me, the excuses would easily flow from my mind that was altered by the alcohol. *Drinking always trumped responsible thinking.* As a direct result of this part of my alcoholism, the outward appearance was that of laziness, and in fact, the reality was laziness. Even with a strong history of an excellent work ethic, I needed to continue to drink above all else. If and when I would show up for work, I was rather good at it! My responsibility of getting there was often interrupted by my desire to drink, which was greater than my desire to do the right thing. Alcoholism transformed me into a slothful person, and that was acceptable because I was drinking. This doesn't make any sense from a point of sobriety today, but I surely lived it then. Does this sound familiar to you?

Envy. Everyone appeared to be on my hit list when I consider envy. When you are needy physically and/or mentally, you see what everyone else has, not what you have. You do not look at those things that are a valuable part of yourself because you cannot see them. When your view is distorted by the effects of alcohol, you look past a beautiful flower and see things that appear to be better at a distance.

How can you not have a feeling of envy? It's natural, from a distorted viewpoint.

You must consider that what you see may not exist the way you see it. Envy creates more envy, causing us to embellish reality. *Our own feelings will always find a way to justify our own feelings!* If I am not right, then who is? Envy will also cause me to want someone or something I will never be entitled to. If someone else has achieved happiness in his marriage, what would make me think I could just insert myself into his life? I must search for my own happiness, my own family. When you are usually drunk, to one degree or another, it's not always easy to see the obvious. Alcoholic thinking is altered and distorted, making it difficult to explain my feelings to someone who is at least reasonably normal. A problem drinker knows what I am saying. He or she has lived it.

Mental uncertainty and confusion. Alcohol is a mind-altering drug, and if you drink it too often or too much, uncertainty and confusion will follow. I often experienced an inability to make a simple decision because I could not think clearly. Then I would try harder, creating even more allusive possibilities to apply in the process of trying to decide. I would drive the simple answer away by muddying up the waters. Confused, I would add more alcohol, finally driving the answer completely from view. Soon I would forget my concern, at least for the time being. I thought drinking gave me clear thinking.

Delusions. The continued, frequent, and excessive use of alcohol (a depressant) will steer our minds into delusions at some point in our drinking years, adding to the progressive effects of alcoholism. These delusions may begin slowly and with moderate symptoms, but they will progress and expand as time and excess goes by.

The minor delusions may be sometimes overlooked or ignored, shrugged off as if not real. Later, the delusions are greater and cannot be ignored. One's reality begins to alter course. I wondered what was real anymore. Where was the line where delusions started, the line that began to emphasize the visions, the line that began to disconnect me from reality? When you are drinking insensately, your blood-alcohol level will fluctuate and blur the lines between your altered realities, sometimes swinging you from one to the other and back again. You are sure you know where you stand, not sure, positive, uncertain again. Delusions begin to change your perception of who you are and what you believe, leaving you staggering mentally, unsure of your footing. Like anything progressive, these symptoms only progress. When too many brain cells are affected, the journey toward permanent mental illness has begun and the road back into recovery becomes littered with obstacles. Some of these obstacles will live with you forever.

Is it time to seek help? Will you have time to turn back?

Grief. This is the largest and most profound of our feelings, and grief affects everyone sometime, somewhere. Here is a brief explanation. The largest category of grief is, of course, the death of someone who is an important part of our lives. Other losses graduate away from our center of influence, depending on our exact relationship and closeness. Other simple losses can bring on the symptoms of grief to lesser degrees. While grief is primarily emotional, it is also physical, cognitive, and philosophical.

When grief occurs during your drinking days, I am sure you would add a drink and try to camouflage your feelings, postponing a proper response. This method may serve you well for the time being but will come back to you in spades! Many recovering alcoholics are still processing their feelings of grief from years past, and they find it more difficult today than it would have been when it first happened.

Try not to postpone a proper reaction to your feelings. Grief will still interrupt our sobriety if it can, but you will find yourself far better prepared to act appropriately and effectively process your feelings while in recovery. Grief can also be felt over the loss of alcohol in your life. Try to stay alert to what these feelings really mean when they begin to encroach in your sober life.

Sadness and depression. We thought all the years of our drinking had delivered all the sadness and depression that could possibly come our way, but we were wrong. In sobriety, our minds clear and memories return at some pretty strange points in time. Not only are we challenged to act in spite of our feelings, we often do not know the origin of our sadness, making it the more difficult to process. If a close friend has passed away, you can celebrate his life with others who mourn along with you, and begin to process the loss. If you're driving to the grocery store and suddenly start to cry for no apparent reason, you can only pull off the road and cry. What next? Where have these feelings come from? What does it mean?

What part of my life, that was on hold, is now ready to come forward in my brain?

Without a quick recollection, the sadness begins to build within and causes depressions without a known source right away. Where do I turn now? One event complicates another and confusion usually results. Before we stopped drinking, we thought this would be a good place to add a drink. Today we know that kind of response only adds problems and solves nothing.

Happiness. Finally, something nice to think about! Happiness is last on my list because it had been forced to be there while I was living and reliving all of my negative emotions. Stop and think about it–happiness cannot push away grieving or any of the many negative feelings we have been dealing with while drinking.

Once we begin to understand our feelings and get them under control, we become free to receive all the happiness that has wanted to be a part of our lives. God did not create us to live without happiness and success. The natural beauty that He bestowed on each of us was always meant to be shared with our loved ones, promoting happiness.

The ability to touch, see, and hear each other in an understanding manner was always His way for us to live. We were never meant to be alone. The most valuable asset in my life is how I feel about others and how they feel about me, not what I may possess. *Happiness when shared creates more happiness!* This is the best conduit to sharing and receiving another one's love. When we are caressing each other, our thoughts do not travel far from the now; we enjoy these moments and feel true happiness that love has created and nourished. While our friendships may not allow for a lot of touching, they do allow for a lot of true feelings. Our warmth and soothing comfort for each other succeeds all other feelings. Happiness is therefore my goal of all recovery plans and should be sought after with passion.

I am happy to say we all deserve it.

CHAPTER 11

Meaningful Friendships in the Fellowship

Our fellowship agrees to honor each other's anonymity, and that is an important facet of the Alcoholics Anonymous program, which allows new members to join without fear of being outed or compromised. In my personal recovery program, I find that I value my friendships above most other aspects of my sober life. Pretty much everyone knows everyone's name, we just don't mention them. Besides, some of the names are Bob with the funny voice, Andy with forty-two years, Bob A., Bob B., Jack S., Jack with the heart, Muscle Mike, Too Tall Terry . . . well, you get the drift. It's easier to just leave the damn names out of the stories, so you will notice that I have not mentioned many by name to protect both the guilty and the innocent.

I could personally write 300 of these stories based on the core of members in my local area who attend the same meetings I do each week. I do a meeting a day for my own enjoyment in different locations and different times, which allows me to cross paths with 300 of my closest friends. Of course, some of these are very casual friends, but some of them are influential in the way I think about important matters in life. I would like you to meet some of my best anonymous friends.

Try to picture a young lady in her early forties, confident, very attractive, and seemingly organized and successful in her own real estate business. Twenty-three years in the program, she volunteers to sponsor about seven new female members at a time, participates in a home group or two each week, chairs meetings when asked, is a speaker at some meetings, sits on the local AA board, supervises the monthly newsletter for our area, coordinates people for chores in our fellowship to keep us up and running, volunteers to support family members of those lost from our groups, holds a pot-luck supper meeting for females each week, and would not be caught dead without her treasured Black Berry. And this is only a snap shot.

She also supports five dogs at home and manages to have a good word and some encouragement for all who cross her path every day. She is lovely to look at and is warm and lov-ing to be around. She plays a critical role of our fellowship and makes me proud just to know her and call her my friend. She has a razor-sharp wit and command of sarcasm as a sec-ond language. She hasn't figured out how to say hello with-out a hug and is also big on texting, not so much time!

For about a year and a half, I had a "meeting mate" who was retired from the New York City Transit Authority, hav-ing spent his working career as a conductor on a subway. He loved AA and considered sobriety precious. He had over thirty-five years sober and loved to tell the story of his spiri-tual awakening that directed him to seek help. He practiced and praised our one-day-at-a-time theory. At seventy-nine years old, he attracted many members in their forties and fif-ties, who were perhaps relating to him as a father figure. All the ladies were drawn to his soft and quiet maturity. We all enjoyed his warm and purely Irish sense of humor.

Upon learning of his lung cancer, he came to me for help and support because of my history and the fact that I had beaten my lung cancer. In his final eight months, I was only able to coach him in dying, not living. His cancer had spread, and he was told he was going to die. All treatments were suspended. His family and friends helped him get to meet-ings until it was no longer physically possible about a week before he surrendered. I held his hand for hours, begging for him to let go just half a day before he died. Never will he be forgotten, never.

My spiritual support person and best friend is critical in helping me keep my head on somewhat straight. For being my closest and most personal friend, she is a married home-maker in her mid-forties (my daughter's age) with a fifteen-year-old son. She is active in our area organization as our secretary and participates regularly in our local meetings. She has also helped me with some of my writings, correcting and editing to aim me in the right direction. Her outward appearance is stunning, almost breathtaking, but her inner warmth and spirituality are her finest traits. She believes that we all need to believe!

She is always cautious for the newer ladies coming into the meetings, coaching them in the right direction while they are getting settled into a routine. She also makes herself available by phone to all the ladies who ask. Although soft-spoken, everyone listens when she contributes to our discussion meetings because of the wisdom she has found in her time in the fellowship. This is another one who could not say hello without an embrace. She spoils me by calling me "treasured friend," a handle I will never release.

One of the men that I look up to in the program is married to a lady also in the program, and at seventy, he enjoys his retirement freedom. They both go to many meetings, both locally and in the cities they visit when seeing their adult children and grandchildren. He has thirty-one years sober, and his wife has twenty-one.

They had met early in life and married only six years ago when they became re-acquainted in the rooms of AA after they had both lost their first spouses. Powerful examples of stability and wisdom make them both outstanding members in high regard. Since he has about twice the sobriety time as me, I like to remind him that he is double my age! We both celebrate our anniversaries in September and belong to the same home group. I am privileged to attend three meetings each week where I enjoy their company and have a special time to chat about personal matters with him when I have questions or concerns. I like to refer to him as my sponsor by ambush!

Next there is a retired lady who arrives early to every meeting to have the chance to talk to a few other members on a more quiet and personal level. Another spiritual lady, she enjoys sharing her experience and her feelings with the people she considers closer to her than her own family. One of her adult sons has chosen to ignore her when she reaches out to him. Even the most profound efforts to restore good-will do not always succeed, and alternative methods will need to be put in place to achieve peace of mind in recovery. This fine lady remains ready to work on family matters, but when things do not go well, she relies on our home group and some of our elders with whom she can relate on a more personal level than at an open meeting. This seems to be the way she has adjusted to her family matters and it's working well for her, another example of adjusting to things we cannot change. We all pray for her personal situation to improve.

On to a fellow whose body had all but given up on him nineteen years ago when he landed in the hospital, one of the worse cases they had ever seen. He had spent years isolating and drinking vast quantities of wine out of several large bottles everyday. His weight was out of control with his organs all starting to fail when he was visited by a couple of old-timers who offered him a chance to recover. When he was finally discharged from the hospital many weeks later and returned to his family home, the old-timers showed up and told him to get in their car for a meeting or go back inside and continue his fatal march. He had five minutes to decide. Thank God he chose to take the hand of Alcoholics Anonymous or he would surely be dead.

Today I see him at a meeting each day, and his stability in sobriety is outstanding. He takes each day and its challenges one at a time. For many months now, he has had to deal with his wife's critical illness, treatments, and care. He has done all this without an inclination of drinking. All of our members listen carefully when he speaks because he is such an outstanding example of implementing the program and changing one's life. He takes his daily work in stride while balancing every other aspect of his life and family in sobriety, including sponsoring several newer members.

I must tell another sad story of a forty-five-year-old lady who died from an unexpected brain aneurysm after many years of successful recovery in AA. She attended two of my weekly meetings and would always amaze me with her complete method of explaining any issue before her. She was a schoolteacher and employed her teaching skills to give us knowledge based on her own experience. Her presentation was always impeccable. She was also active in sponsoring newer women coming into the program, was fully involved in her synagogue, a busy member of her neighborhood and community, and was highly regarded by all of her students past and present. I used to enjoy kidding her about stealing my thoughts on a subject because when she was through explaining it, there was little else that could be said! She was a strikingly attractive young woman, humorous, and pleasant to be around. I wish that I could report that sobriety solves every problem, but it is still just the foundation for future life that we may be allowed.

I am not convinced that death is the end of it for all of us. Two months after this woman's funeral, one of her co-workers paused at their school to look at the drawings and memories posted in the hallway by the teacher's former students. While the co-worker was there, she felt a presence and called out her friend's name. A chill ran down her spine and she was aware of that moving presence while she stood alone for several minutes. I think that our friend is now only a whisper away.

There is a very quiet Vietnam veteran in his early sixties who usually arrives fashionably late and sits in the back of the rooms. I have known him for over two years but know little about him because of his quietness, which is not to say he doesn't have friends in the fellowship. I understand his posture. I lived part of the hell that permeates his thoughts. I have been uncomfortable to pry. He rarely speaks at meetings, but he has disclosed that his drinking brought him to a place where he had the barrel of a gun in his mouth. A really close call. His sobriety continues with honor years after that incident. *Please* don't forget our Vietnam vets!

Sometimes you can learn valuable lessons from the newer members, as well as the more seasoned ones. I have greatly enjoyed a newer female member who is raising four children alone. Her wisdom and maturity defy her early-forties age, but all of her stories about her life and family now draw my complete attention.

Her oldest child of fifteen has become a *sobriety coach,* amazing when you consider her age and the amount of love that motivates her. Every time she tells a family-related story, I relate to her even though my kids are in their forties. She delivers powerful messages of hope, love, and family values that teach us all many lessons.

Old-timers with over twenty-five years of sobriety tell some of the most colorful stories that you really cannot forget. One such fellow in his late sixties, who goes to several of my scheduled weekly meetings, recalls an astounding story while he was drinking with an army buddy years ago. My friend who was a mechanic on a helicopter, and his friend who was a pilot, got themselves pretty well liquored up one day and wanted to go to a far away fishing spot they both liked. Well, the writing is on the wall. Off they flew, and when they returned with their catch, their commanding officer was waiting with the suggestion that my friend consider letting his term of service expire shortly and leave on good terms, or face court-martial for his part in all this. That concluded his time in the service.

Today he is wrestling with dialysis three times a week, caring for his wife who is undergoing chemotherapy and radiation treatments, and making his meetings whenever possible. He knows full well what drinking did to him, and he now takes one day at a time being responsible to himself and his family. It is a pleasure to know someone like this because of his humility and honesty in the program. When he needs help, he is not bashful about picking up the phone to call a fellow.

Our coffee maker and set-up person at one of my meetings was a real estate salesperson for many years while raising a family in the suburbs. After she retired, her drinking increased and she became secretive and cunning in keeping her daily supplies in her home/drinking place. It is hard to be careful of people, places, and things when this is your method of drinking. In her three-plus years of recovery, she has been an outspoken member of our fellowship, helping many to understand these difficult circumstances. Her infectious enthusiasm for our recovery method has helped many others, and she continues to carry the message at every meeting she attends.

It is rewarding to watch her succeed in avoiding the pitfalls of an affluent lifestyle that could have secretly killed her. Often the well-to-do can afford to control their drinking circumstances to a point of no return. Remember that we deal with a cunning and baffling disease that searches for ways to hide itself inside of our lives.

To get into recovery is to escape certain harm. To stay in recovery displays honest and courageous thinking and an acceptance of our disease that will lead us to a better life. We all experience turning points in our lives that cannot be overlooked.

Here's another sad ending. Because he has passed, I will tell you that I nicknamed this fellow Jell-O Man. An aristocratic gentleman of seventy-one years with an astounding and colorful history of world travels and relationships, including many philanthropic endeavors, was one of us who one day fetched up in a detoxification center shaking uncontrollably. Alcohol is the ultimate equalizer.

His story went on to tell us that the attending nurses felt that the only thing they thought he would be able to hold down was, you guessed it: Jell-O. Well, Jell-O Man was hilariously animated in describing how the Jell-O cubes went flying in every direction when he tried to get some of it down. I like to think they are still scraping that stuff off the ceilings, and when I press my memory, I can see an odd color still decorating his hair.

Rectal cancer, procedures, and treatments would occupy his final twelve weeks before medical complications quieted our laughter. He was an outstanding and imposing figure of a man. We who had the pleasure to know him will all remember him with great affection. You just know when someone is headed to a better place.

Go in peace, my friend.

Not all of our members choose to stay in the program for various reasons. I would like to describe two of them in the recent history of my group. A forty-one-year-old mother of two girls, divorced and a homeowner with a full-time job stayed in our meetings for about eight months before declaring that she felt her ability to control her drinking had somehow returned. During the last year, she has been successful in finding a really great boyfriend, staying away from any drinking problems, and has succeeded in starting her own business. I pray every day that if any problems return to her that she knows where we are, and what to do. This is a program for those who want it, not need it. We all wish her the best in her future.

The second is a fellow of fifty-five years who had a long history of deep and complicated physical, mental, and spiritual problems. He spent many years in the program and the fellowship until his problems drew him away from our meetings, which lead to his return to drinking and drugs. Historically known for his intense humor and talent, there was also a dark side. As he got away from our meetings and his personal contacts, his problems overshadowed his real life. Sadly, he took his own life in a deliberate manner. I believe it is of no value to differentiate between suicide or accidental overdose that leads to one's death. The tragic result is the same. Another permanent solution to a temporary problem, no matter how great the problem appears. Here I can only pray that his death will be a message for our fellowship that will help someone down the road. No man's life should ever go unnoticed. We are all too important in the eyes of God.

A story of courage within our ranks. A short but very fit man in his late sixties, who was a veteran and a fellow known for scrapping when he drank, now enjoys his retirement between

New York and Florida. He is an active motorcycle enthusiast and a daily meeting maker who loves his dogs. Gruff on the outside, he is a warm and sensitive gentleman on the inside. He recently suffered a massive stroke, disabling his left side and temporarily affecting his vision. When he completes his rehabilitation in a few weeks, he expects to return to his independent way of life. While hospitalized, many of his friends from the fellowship have visited and kept him company as he progresses along his new road. His long-term sobriety and strong mental attitude are helping him overcome this temporary condition. He had also been a weight lifter and bodybuilder, which I am sure has been helpful. He will be back in our fellowship soon as strong as ever, no doubt!

Another real estate salesperson still working part-time in the office of a Realtor enjoys about five years in sobriety and is a central figure in the affairs of one of my weekly meetings. Her attributes include regularly giving rides to members who have not received their licenses back yet, setting up our meeting weekly, and baking the best snacks ever! Her outspoken manner is notable, and I find she is usually directly on point. She can do a crossword puzzle while I'm fixing my coffee and grabbing some of the snacks. Alcoholics are some of the brightest people on the planet, and it is fascinating to listen to their logic and experiences at, before, or after our gatherings. This woman will keep you on your toes mentally during a friendly conversation.

She is a great friend who always arrives early to share with those of us who seek a comfortable fellowship before our meetings get filled up with other members. It's kind of a personal meeting before the formal meeting, a plan I can recommend easily and a great way to get to know some other people with the same problems or situations you are dealing with. Before the meetings are a relatively quiet time for those of us who have hearing or speech problems. I find that it adds meaning and depth to my experience. It's more personal.

When I find someone who makes me think, I like to spend a bit more time with them. Once a week at an early morning meeting at the local community center, I have the privilege to sit beside someone I look up to. His reason for arriving early is to set up the chairs for the meeting and reserve his favorite spot in the room. My reason is to claim the seat next to him and be able to spend some quiet time talking about anything. As the room fills with people, I lose the ability to make myself heard due to my frog-like voice. I don't remember us having a lot of recovery talk, but we enjoy diverse and lively conversations, usually with slightly different opinions.

This fellow started out as a successful attorney and is currently working as a law clerk for a local firm. His alcoholism cost him greatly with regard to his career and family.

His experiences are interesting to listen to, and he is one of the most well-read friends I have ever had. No matter the topic, he is usually ready with a learned opinion.

We also enjoy the company of a gentleman who joins us seasonally from his rehabilitation center that he owns in the West. He has a gazillion years in the program and is on top of the recovery business, but he likes to summer in upstate New York near the horse track of fame in Saratoga Springs. He arrives early at the meeting to bring snacks (you may see a connection here) and sits with us in the front of the meeting room because he has trouble hearing.

There we all are in the summer; can't hear well, can't talk well, and won't stop talking until he hears an objection. That's the three of us. As the room fills to capacity, as it always does, we listen and comment when it seems appropriate and possible. It is a personal challenge to stay abreast of these guys, but I would not miss our Saturday mornings for anything. Our friendship is real, important, and supportive to our collective sobriety of about seventy-eight years. These are two of the most informative hours I experience each week. The fellowship is infectious.

Being an old fart is not a requirement of the fellowship, but it helps you to fit in.

Some of our members are actually in their teens and twenties. One young lady comes to mind who is currently working on an advanced degree at a local college.

In her early twenties, she is a picture of youth and energy. Being interested in her history, I made a point to attend an "away meeting" where she was scheduled to speak in a nearby town. She was powerful in her presentation intended to help newer members identify with her, and she stayed on point for the entire half hour of her talk. I noticed that most of the time she stared at her painted hands, a result of her artistry. When she finished sharing very personal, heart-wrenching stories meant only to help others, she seemed to open up and begin to smile widely. All during her talk I could hear sounds of approval and signs of agreement and understanding for everything she had shared. She was given a lot of well-deserved applause for a job well done. I enjoyed seeing her recognize her acceptance from the room full of members. It is good to watch people grow in their sobriety. Most of us recognize the importance of steady progress. It is great to see this happening in our younger contingent because they have so many years ahead of them to grow and experience life in a full and sober way.

One of my friends in his upper sixties discovered he had some blockages in his heart last year and readily made the arrangements to have the recommended bypass procedure because he felt it was the right thing to do for his family. He faced his problems with no fear. After the triple bypass, he was discharged to his home to continue in his recovery. There he developed pneumonia and was readmitted to our local hospital for treatment. Then, a mysterious infection attacked his system, causing him to slip into a coma. The intensive care unit worked on him for over eight weeks until he finally stabilized unexpectedly. The nurses I had talked to cautioned me to expect the worst along the way, but there he was again, ready to go for rehabilitation at another hospital. About four weeks later, he emerged weak but ready to aid in his personal recovery. Now three months later, he is again cheerful and happily living with a new expression on his lips: *It is what it is!* I believe sobriety adds so much to our lives that we are capable of overcoming long odds. I count him on my "borrowed time" list.

There is also a nurse I watched get sober in the rooms, who spent her first year dealing with problems from her husband who seemed to feel like he lost his drinking partner, rather than gaining a sober wife. These real-life situations can happen, and they become a burden to further complicate our strides to get sober and stay sober. I saw this lady in her mid-forties struggle and hang on through her first year, gaining the strength to learn that she could overcome her marital issues and continue to stay sober and work the program that created changes she needed in her life in order to survive. She continues to do well another year after her first anniversary and seems to smile a lot more now. Building on our daily successes gives us the strength to overcome new challenges when they may occur. Hanging on one day at a time is worth it in the long run.

Well, this storyline never really ends. There are millions of recovering people in Alcoholics Anonymous, literally from every walk of life. Alcoholism has no known boundaries. On a short list of occupations that I know are doctors, nurses, medical technicians, counselors, judges, lawyers, singers, actors, musicians, poets, writers, journalists, artists, rehabilitation workers and owners, salespeople of every description, food service workers and experts, horsemen, historians, accountants, insurance people, real estate folks, mechanics, and yes, politicians. What you are doesn't matter; who you are does. If you are an alcoholic, there is something you can do.

I wanted to share the stories of some of my friends to demonstrate the diversity of people I deal with daily and to give you an idea of some of the struggles they have to deal with in their recovery. If you know someone in recovery, I trust that you will encourage them and reinforce the benefits of continued sobriety. If you are in recovery, God bless you, and I encourage you to hang on. One of the first people I met in Alcoholics Anonymous used to say insensately: *It just keeps getting better!* I wanted to strangle anyone who told me that. But, at the end of the day, he was right. The blessings I have received are countless and precious. I would not have dreamed of all that I am blessed with today. My life is full of sobriety and all of its rewards. If I can do it, you can do it.

Near the end of their lives, the founders of AA were asked if they would change anything about AA or the book *Alcoholics Anonymous*, which has been out nearly seventy-five years now. Their answer was a surprising yes. They would have changed the first word in the fifth chapter, "How it Works," from *rarely* to *never*!

"Never have we seen a person fail who has thoroughly followed our path." If there is any secret to AA, that's it. Everyone who thoroughly follows our path can succeed. There is no room for failure if you can follow the map to success. Letting go of our old ideas, and letting God lead the way today, will be rewarded.

CHAPTER 12

Hodgepodge, Conclusions, and Credits

One of the most important things I learned in early recovery was that alcohol was a drug and *I was an addict.* When you have lost control of any substance, you are demonstrating your addiction to it. *Get over it!* To ignore this reality is to prolong your suffering until you possibly reach a point of no return. There are several such destinations, like wet brain syndrome, irreversible diseases of your internal organs, unintended death, or suicide caused by depression and/or accidental overdose. It is important to know that these things can occur through the use and abuse of alcohol or any other drug, or easily by some combination of substances. When someone is under the influence of substances, that is exactly the time when the addict is working all of their angles to promote continued use of that medication and the profound numbing of their feelings and their perceived easing of difficulties. When someone thinks their drug is helping them, it is hard for them to just walk away from it. They will try to justify their behaviors. The problem with this pattern is that *addiction equals death* if left untreated.

The only unknowns in this assertion are the time line and the gory details. Most responsible adults should be aware of this phenomenon if they are actively a part of our society and are paying any attention to our socioeconomic condition. Not all alcohol- or drug-related deaths are clearly reported. More likely, they will be rumored. We need to expand our base of information in order to allow a clearer picture to develop within our communities concerning the frequency and numbers of these types of deaths. There are significantly more than we know about.

Obituaries are usually written by families and should not be read as if they are fact. ("Died at home, unexpectedly, after a brief illness," etcetera.) In my opinion, some other way needs to be developed to report the statistics about overdose suicides or accidents while at the same time protecting the families. The public would be better off knowing how often these events are affecting the community and endangering their own families and neighbors. By disclosing the actual numbers, the community would be made aware of the extent of this problem all around them. I do not believe that families have the right to protect their privacy if their privacy leads to an unknown number of additional deaths that may have been forewarned. Wouldn't it be rewarding to know that our loss was the key to helping others on the brink of disaster? Suicide is a frequent consequence of addiction, possibly because of the secrecy we attach to it.

I also question why we are so reluctant to intervene and try to change the course of events certain to descend on any alcoholic or addict close to us. Do we really believe that bad things won't happen to people we love? How many self-serving excuses can we come up with to avoid confrontation and the possibility of tarnishing our close relationships? Lack of action will slow, diminish, or postpone the start of recovery, or at least the start of another period where drugs and/or alcohol are stopped in favor of seeking a solution. If you make a mistake here, you may well end up mourning a loss, and *forever* questioning yourself about your lack of action. Life and the pursuit of happiness are far more valuable. Temporarily tarnishing a relationship will mend, or not. Death doesn't get any better. I'm serious.

I would ask you to remember Marilyn Monroe, Elvis Presley, or the now infamous Anna Nicole Smith, to name just a few. Being rich, talented, famous, or some combination thereof, seems to enable the addiction and the disasters that lie ahead.

Inaction or acceptance leads to isolation by the dying person from meaningful help because they are able to control their circumstances enough to not be diverted from their mission of certain death. If they are not rich or powerful, they would just have to be smarter, and I can tell you I have never met a stupid addict. In fact, addiction attracts some of the smartest and most talented people on the planet. I can't even talk casually about some of the people I know in the program because of their international fame. They would be recognized easily and their anonymity blown, not something AA would endorse.

Current media is also guilty of glorifying the drinking escapades of some young and famous personalities, going so far as to suggest that this behavior can make our children rich and successful. Our young people respond to this kind of rubbish and hold it to be true as they begin to experience life, while exposing themselves to the possibility of alcohol and/or drug use because of their beliefs. When will our nationwide value system begin to reflect decency and reasonable behaviors?

Returning to my assertions that what causes a problem is the problem, and it's important to stay off the damn elevator are valuable tools to maintain sobriety while keeping a level head. If these are the only things learned from my work, I will rest in peace.

Alcohol and drugs *are* the problem and cannot be any part of a successful plan of recovery. You must control the alcoholic well enough to focus on that point and not be convinced otherwise. Agreeing with an addict who wants to "cut down on their use" as a solution to the current "problems" simply postpones their death. Addicts can't control their use based on some promise of limiting our habits. The addict or alcoholic can throw 101 excuses at you to the contrary without needing time to think about it, and none of these excuses are valid. The effects of drugs and/or alcohol chemically and insanely justify the continued use to the addicts way of thinking, so he or she can continue to medicate him or herself, while satisfying and repelling the people trying to save his or her life. If you win this tug-of-war, they win.

For your information, the massive drinking of alcohol can result in alcoholic poisoning at the earliest, or organ death in due time. The mixing of drugs and alcohol yields results that even a chemist would be unable to quantify or predict the effective outcome of. *Addiction is insidious,* and to allow it to continue is like letting someone pull the trigger of a gun without knowing where it is pointed. It is easier to get someone's attention when they are bemoaning their "problems" such as legal issues, physical problems, social dysfunctions, work problems, etcetera. Our first priority is to focus on the only real problem, which is the drinking or drug abusing. When we eliminate the real problem by beginning a plan of recovery, all the other problems will melt away with only cursory attention. *Focus on the real problem!*

On a personal level, if you think you know how much your addict is drinking or drugging, you are dead wrong. Addicts do not disclose the exact amount of their use for two reasons: One, they don't want you to know, and two, they probably don't know themselves. If you press the issue, they will probably give you a drug-affected answer, and it will in no way be accurate. Besides, the resulting effects are what matters, not how much it took to get them there. Time changes this equation anyway, as time will also change the tolerance levels from person to person, substance to substance, and is of no real importance in anything other than illustrating the resulting effects. This detail may make the story more interesting, but it will not help in any way to get someone sober.

What concerns me the most are the people closest to the addict who are likely to understand the addict who has their finger on the trigger. Would you pull the trigger yourself? Inaction allows continued deepening addiction, which still equals death. Death may not be the first consequence of addiction, but it will not be denied in the normal course of events. What part of this do you think not important? We stand at a turning point of someone's life, and it is more likely that we will have to initiate some kind of recovery plan. It is difficult to be in this position, but someone has to make a sound decision. It will not come from a drug-affected mind.

Alcoholics Anonymous is a fellowship of highly experienced drinkers. The bond and understanding created is unprecedented. We are not only familiar with all the stories and excuses; we were the ones who first made them up. It is impossible to fool a room full of fools. We use our experience to encourage newcomers to get real and give AA a reasonable try. In maintaining our own sobriety, we must be responsible to pass on this message of hope to those who seek help after our own arrival in the fellowship. It is a program of attraction, not promotion. "If you want what we have, and are willing to go to any lengths to get it, then you are ready to take certain steps . . ." These are some of the words that resound at every AA meeting being held across the world today, as an introduction and encouragement to all of our members young and old, new to the program or seasoned veteran.

The fellowship is ripe with outstanding characters with hearts as big as all outdoors. The caring and devotion can be felt before, during, and after every meeting from these people. If the newcomers can hang in there for just a short time, they will begin to understand our mission, see the way it works, and want to become an active member themselves. Some of the members I talk to, and more importantly, listen to each day have over thirty years of continuous sobriety under their belts. They have no reason to pull any punches. They are usually basic and straightforward people with immeasurable compassion for those who need their help in learning how to stay sober one day at a time. You should never be embarrassed to openly recommend Alcoholics Anonymous to someone you think could use that program and fellowship. It could be the most important thing you ever do. It's a lot easier than pulling someone out of a burning house, but the result is the same. Another life and another family protected from grief.

Several years after my lung cancer operation, I asked my primary-care doctor how long he really thought I might live, since I had pretty much accepted that I was living on borrowed time by then. He said when he first learned of the nature and scope of my cancer and the radical operation, his first impression was that I would survive only four months or so because of the type of cancer, which was complicated by multiple lymph node involvement.

Now, over ten years later, well beyond active alcoholism, three heart attacks, two heart failures, lung cancer to include the removal of my entire right lung, ongoing treatment of congestive heart failure along with the implantation of the cardiac device for pacing and as a defibrillator, he said he now is thinking I am going to live forever! I like a man with a sense of humor. No matter when the final curtain comes down, I know that life has been more than I expected, and I can assure you, more than I deserved. With all in consideration, I have learned to live one day at a time, trying to suck all the good out of each day I am granted. My greatest rewards include my family relationships, my friends, and the ability to attend Alcoholics Anonymous in an effort to give back.

The true feelings of love and affection I experience every day keep me alive and encourage the next meeting where I can share my experience, strength, and hope in an effort to pass along my most precious gift: sobriety. Trust me when I tell you, I can see and feel when others begin to understand this simple program for complicated people. Their looks actually change, their posture is different as they stand a little taller, their smiles broaden, and their eyes sparkle for the first time since they stopped drinking. They begin to say things that sound familiar, and they mean it. What a pleasure it is to see the personal growth of others and the permanent relief of their problems, *one day at a time.*

Unfortunately, the pains of real life have dampened my enthusiasm, with events like the loss of my sister over three years ago now, and since, the loss of five more of my friends. Getting sober is the beginning of a new life, not the answer to all prayers and the solution to everything. Life is still going to happen; not all of it is going to be good. Reality tells me that life is life, and we are supposed to be able to cope with whatever is given to us to handle, with the help of one's Higher Power. I call on Him everyday now. I know He listens. I have felt His Angels and I am living His rewards.

To the best of my knowledge and memory, the loss of my only sister was the cruelest of all emotions I have ever experienced in my life, and yet I never once considered picking up a drink to help me through this time. I took the pain and love her more now as each day passes. She was so proud of my sobriety. I can also love myself for trying my best to stay sober no matter what the problem or issue that may confront me. Adding a drink to a problem would only complicate the problem and create new problems. Very big and possibly fatal problems.

Working the steps of the Alcoholics Anonymous program has embedded in me the values needed to live a better life while maintaining sobriety. The longer I go without a drink, the stronger I become in managing my life. Today I can feel the values at work in my daily life, and I respond consciously and feel proud deep inside of myself. The most important thing is for me to be able to trust myself for the first time in my life. My experiences clearly demonstrate that AA works and everything else fails over time. You can take it from me and my friends, or you can continue to challenge fate like the many who have not been able to maintain sobriety, while they try to reinvent the wheel and protect their right to drink.

The dangers of continued problem drinking and the progression that is relentless will always be there, until you can surrender your will according to the tenets of this spiritual and blessed program. The only thing you have to lose is all the bad stuff, so go to a meeting, close your mouth, open your ears, and you will grow beyond all expectations. You won't be the new guy for long, and the rewards you will reap are well beyond your wildest dreams. I wish you well.

"My name is Bob Allen and I am an alcoholic!"

Afterword

In accordance with the twelfth step of the Alcoholics Anonymous program, which asks me to carry the message to others who still suffer, I have written this book. I hope if you have been helped in any way or informed by my story, that you get your butt to a meeting and ask for help. I also want you to realize that *what causes the problem is the problem* and that *the alcoholic elevator only has a down button, so stay the hell off it*! In addition, there are no escalators to sobriety; *you're going to have to take the steps.*

When you do find the humility to finally ask for help, it will be the greatest feeling you have ever had, and I promise it will help erase all of the other feelings I listed except happiness and love. When you finally surrender; the battle will be yours. There is a world of possibilities ahead for you if you take the pain now, claim your seat in the rooms of AA, and learn to live sober.

We all still have the right to drink, but that right does not need to be acted upon or caressed. We should all simply decide *not to drink today and go to a meeting.* If that doesn't work for you, *go to a meeting today and don't drink.* When you hear someone repeatedly saying, "It just keeps getting better," try to resist the urge to strangle the living crap out of him. You will learn that he is completely correct and is accurately predicting the life that is rushing toward you. Peace and love.

Special Memories, and Acknowledgments

I would like to dedicate this book to my sister-in-law Virginia Hunt, whose faith and spirituality have caused me to look deeply within myself and to reflect on a lifetime of events and observations. Her openness and persistence have persuaded me to share my experience in a hope someone might learn something without having to walk in my shoes for over six decades. My core belief, in a perfect world, is that we should all be issued experience upon our birth and then be required to actually apply it in our lives. Failing that, I guess we will have to read books. I am not the last authority on these subjects, but as she points out, my view of these matters are at least fresh. I have the greatest respect for "Ginny" and thank her for her encouragement.

Special memories go to my beautiful sister, Judith Dorcas Joyce, whose life was a testament to everyone who crossed her path. "Dork" remained grounded in reality throughout her life and was always proving her points of view with great homespun humor. Her compounded illnesses shortened her life to less than sixty-five years, forcing her to become the Guardian Angel of her first grandchild when he was only a few days old. My only sibling in now *just a whisper away* and has unwittingly contributed to these pages. My love for her continues to grow and if you ever hear "Ya think?" she is not far away.

I must certainly acknowledge my loving wife, Betty Boop, who has survived my experiences and has supported me through thick and thin for over twenty-one years. She must also be credited with filling in several blanks for me when I was otherwise unconscious. Her love and commitment are beyond words. Her devotion is simply unexplainable.

I also have to mention a past supervisor, Aaron Butler, who changed my nickname from BA to OBT (On Borrowed Time) in 1998, and a fellow salesperson, Alan Rogers, who picked up the gauntlet in 2004 when I fetched up at the last store I was going to work for. These guys helped me keep it real since there was no good explanation for me to still be sucking air. If you don't joke about these things, life gets way too serious. Also deserving of honorable mention are, Bill W. and Dr. Bob, who developed Alcoholics Anonymous seventy-five years ago, and their millions of current friends. They have all taught me volumes of unforgettable stuff and allowed me the time I needed to bring it all together for myself, finding my chair in the meetings. I, like many of us, was a slow learner. A key in my life was the rekindling of the spirituality Alcoholics Anonymous promoted within me. Life is now good!

When all else fails (and it will), turn to Alcoholics Anonymous!

Bob Allen

(BA/OBT)

"This is the end of the book, and the beginning of a new life . . ."

CPSIA information can be obtained at www.ICGtesting.com
Printed in the USA
LVOW091813210612

287115LV00010B/126/P